NEW DIRECTIONS FOR TEACHING AND LEARNING

Robert J. Menges, *Northwestern University*
EDITOR-IN-CHIEF

Marilla D. Svinicki, *University of Texas, Austin*
ASSOCIATE EDITOR

Developing Senior Faculty as Teachers

Martin J. Finkelstein
Seton Hall University

Mark W. LaCelle-Peterson
State University of New York, Geneseo

EDITORS

Number 55, Fall 1993

JOSSEY-BASS PUBLISHERS
San Francisco

DEVELOPING SENIOR FACULTY AS TEACHERS
Martin J. Finkelstein, Mark W. LaCelle-Peterson (eds.)
New Directions for Teaching and Learning, no. 55
Robert J. Menges, Editor-in-Chief
Marilla D. Svinicki, Associate Editor

LC 85-644763   ISSN 0271-0633   ISBN 1-55542-682-4

NEW DIRECTIONS FOR TEACHING AND LEARNING is part of The Jossey-Bass Higher and Adult Education Series and is published quarterly by Jossey-Bass Inc., Publishers, 350 Sansome Street, San Francisco, California 94104-1342. Second-class postage paid at San Francisco, California, and at additional mailing offices. POSTMASTER: Send address changes to New Directions for Teaching and Learning, Jossey-Bass Inc., Publishers, 350 Sansome Street, San Francisco, California 94104-1342.

SUBSCRIPTIONS for 1993 cost $45.00 for individuals and $60.00 for institutions, agencies, and libraries.

EDITORIAL CORRESPONDENCE should be sent to Robert J. Menges, Northwestern University, Center for the Teaching Professions, 2003 Sheridan Road, Evanston, Illinois 60208-2610.

Cover photograph by Richard Blair/Color & Light   © 1990.

Manufactured in the United States of America. Nearly all Jossey-Bass books, jackets, and periodicals are printed on recycled paper that contains at least 50 percent recycled waste, including 10 percent postconsumer waste. Many of our materials are also printed with vegetable-based ink; during the printing process these inks emit fewer volatile organic compounds (VOCs) than petroleum-based inks. VOCs contribute to the formation of smog.

CONTENTS

EDITORS' NOTES

Through the 1990s colleges and universities will experience major changes, already begun, in two areas: the diversity of their student bodies and the age of their core faculty. The demographic picture regarding students could not be clearer: the student body will continue to grow increasingly diverse in terms of ethnicity, cultural background, economic status, and academic preparedness. More and more students will come from the groups that have been least well-served by higher education in the past—groups who have entered higher education in low proportions, and have dropped out in high proportions (Levine and Associates, 1989). If all students are to succeed in higher education, as historically they have not, then college teaching will need to change in some fundamental ways. Compelling evidence suggests that student retention and ultimate success depends, in part, on the ability of professors—most of whom have been teaching for many years—to provide appropriate classroom experiences and learning assistance (Richardson and Skinner, in press; Treisman, 1985).

Faculty demographics are equally clear and present a stark contrast: the professoriate, mostly white (89 percent) and male (73 percent), will continue to age as the large cohort of faculty hired in the expansion decades of the 1960s and early 1970s reaches mid- and late career. According to the U.S. Department of Education (1990), more than half of all full-time faculty members in 1988 were over age forty-five, nearly two-thirds had tenure, and relatively few between the ages of forty-five and sixty anticipated leaving their current position. Clearly, the faculty members who will face the challenges and opportunities of the college classroom in the 1990s will be a seasoned, stable, and—since most are tenured—job-secure cohort. While the students are changing, the faculty remain the same.

If today's senior faculty members have years of active service ahead of them, they will, nonetheless, eventually begin to retire. Indeed, within the next decade and a half higher education will face a relative *shortage* of faculty and once again hire large numbers of new faculty members (Crawley, 1990; Bowen and Schuster, 1986). Today's senior faculty members will do much of the hiring and most of the socializing of this next generation that will ultimately take their place. The 1990s are therefore crucial to the long-term prospects of U.S. higher education.

Preparation for this eventual turnover in the faculty ranks must include consideration of how today's senior faculty can provide the models, the supporting policies, and the appropriate reward structures to socialize tomorrow's new faculty into the teaching role. Seen in this scope, the effort amounts to more than the sum of individuals' isolated labors: it entails the creation of positive teaching environments. Yet relatively little is known

either about how senior faculty are tackling the day-to-day teaching challenges of the 1990s or about how institutions can create optimal environments to support them in the effort.

If senior faculty members in their last decades of professional service do, in fact, turn their collective energies to improving teaching and learning, the potential for long-term impact on collegiate education is tremendous. Engaging senior faculty, who control the rewards structure, in reflection on how excellent teaching is best supported can fundamentally alter institutional priorities toward a more appropriate balance between teaching and research—toward a better teaching environment.

Prospects for Developing Positive Teaching Environments

Prospects for success in this endeavor depend on the interest of senior faculty and the readiness of campuses, about which previous research only hints. As to faculty readiness to engage in the development of positive teaching climates, the evidence is mixed. Some consider the current "aging of the professoriate" as an obstacle to improving teaching. Much research on senior faculty, for example, emphasizes administrators' fears that faculty vitality decreases with age (see review by Caffarella, Armour, Fuhrman, and Wergin, 1989). Edgerton (1990) notes that today's senior faculty were hired in a period when socialization to the teaching role took the back seat to other, seemingly more immediate concerns, like building enough classrooms to house burgeoning enrollments and publishing so as not to "perish." If senior faculty did not focus on teaching early in their careers, are they likely to do so now when the pressure is off?

Other data, however, suggest a more positive outlook. According to the Carnegie Foundation for the Advancement of Teaching (1989), fully 71 percent of faculty report that teaching is their primary interest. Even at research universities, a significant proportion of faculty are as committed to teaching as to research (Gray, Froh, and Diamond, 1992). Studies that bring the perspective of adult development theory to bear on faculty development show that faculty generally turn their attention away from research and more toward teaching over the course of their careers (Baldwin and Blackburn, 1981). Evidence is clear that interest in teaching is high among current faculty members, and that among senior faculty members in particular the interest tends to increase over the course of their careers (El-Khawas, 1991). How that interest is or could be expressed remain unanswered questions.

Evidence about institutional readiness is sketchy. Despite public commitment to teaching, and despite strong faculty interest, the current campus climate is not widely perceived to support a faculty focus on teaching. The very study that found most faculty to be more interested in teaching than in research reported that 77 percent believed that their *institution* valued research more than teaching. It would appear, then, that current American fac-

ulty, including senior faculty, are ready to focus on teaching, but perceive their campuses to be inhospitable climates for that endeavor. In order to transform collegiate teaching in the 1990s, we need to understand how senior faculty—those tenured faculty in the middle and later stages of their careers who now dominate higher education—develop as teachers, and what institutions can do to encourage and support them.

Organization of This Volume

The chapters assembled for this volume represent major research and intervention efforts that can inform faculty developers and academic administrators as they seek to develop new programs and initiatives. The ideas generated here will also benefit department heads and deans by providing an overview of the career concerns and needs of senior faculty, as well as strategies to address those needs.

The first three chapters focus on research. In Chapter One, Rice and Finkelstein review the academic career development of senior faculty through a synthesis of the research literature, an analysis of data on senior faculty extracted from recent national surveys, and an elaboration of recently developed models of the "new American scholar." In Chapter Two, LaCelle-Peterson and Finkelstein report on an intensive examination of the teaching careers and practices of 111 senior faculty with a focus on the support role of the employing college or university. In Chapter Three, Boice reports on a comparative analysis of middle-aged disillusioned faculty with a comparison group of exemplary senior faculty at three universities. From that analysis, two things emerge: a portrait of four fault lines in the etiology of midcareer faculty disillusionment, and some lessons learned and implications for addressing the issues of that subgroup productively.

The next four chapters describe model programs and intervention strategies for senior faculty. In Chapter Four, Farmer distills the lessons learned during a ten-year effort to comprehensively redesign the reward system at a liberal arts college, including a senior faculty peer review system that builds upon a five-year individual professional growth plan, and a voluntary performance-based compensation system that provides additional merit pay for faculty who have reached the top step of their salary scale. In Chapter Five, Braid describes a faculty-administrative coalition that emerged at a private urban commuter campus to redesign the freshman year experience. Building on curriculum models drawn from the college honors program, and leveraging funds from multiple external sources, the effort drew 40 percent of the full-time faculty into curricular and pedagogical renewal initiatives. In Chapter Six, Jackson and Simpson describe the design of a yearlong seminar experience designed to involve senior faculty in the planning and delivery of introductory-level courses. Eight fellows annually have been working with junior faculty, teaching assistants, and staff of the campus instructional

improvement center to improve the quality of instruction and student learning at the introductory levels.

The final chapters provide a "larger" perspective on senior faculty. In Chapter Seven, Smith and Smith focus on interinstitutional, cooperative approaches to developing and sustaining a focus on teaching among senior faculty in delimited geographic regions. Two distinct institutional models are presented: in Washington, an interinstitutional network developed out of grass-roots faculty initiatives and was later given sustained state support; and in New Jersey, state concern over support for faculty development led to the creation of an independent, campus-based institute with a unique statewide, intersector charge. In Chapter Eight, Finkelstein and Jemmott distill the lessons of earlier chapters, framing the plight and the promise of senior faculty as metaphorically that of the "village elder"—full of untapped promise. In the concluding appendix, Seal compiles an annotated list of resources that can guide administrators, faculty developers, and faculty themselves as they seek to design effective institutional interventions to enhance the work and careers of senior faculty.

Martin J. Finkelstein
Mark W. LaCelle-Peterson
Editors

References

Baldwin, R. G., and Blackburn, R. T. "The Academic Career as a Developmental Process." *Journal of Higher Education*, 1981, 52, 598–614.

Bowen, H. R., and Schuster, J. *American Professors*. New York: Oxford University Press, 1986.

Caffarella, R. S., Armour, R. A., Fuhrman, B. S., and Wergin, J. F. "Mid-Career Faculty: Refocusing the Perspective." *Review of Higher Education*, 1989, 12 (4), 403–410.

Carnegie Foundation for the Advancement of Teaching. *The Condition of the Professoriate: Attitudes and Trends, 1989*. Princeton, N.J.: Carnegie Foundation for the Advancement of Teaching, 1989.

Crawley, A. L. "Meeting the Challenge of an Aging Professoriate: An Opportunity for Leadership." *To Improve the Academy*, 1990, 10, 231–243.

Edgerton, R. "The Teaching Initiative." *To Improve the Academy*, 1990, 10, 191–197.

El-Khawas, E. "Senior Faculty in Academe: Active, Committed to the Teaching Role." *Research Briefs*, 1991, 2 (5), 1.

Gray, P. J., Froh, R. C., and Diamond, R. M. *On the Balance Between Research and Undergraduate Teaching: A National Study of Research Universities*. Syracuse, N.Y.: Center for Instructional Development, 1992.

Levine, A., and Associates. *Shaping Higher Education's Future: Demographic Realities and Opportunities, 1990–2000*. San Francisco: Jossey-Bass, 1989.

Richardson, R. C., and Skinner, E. F. *Achieving Access and Quality: Case Studies in Equity*. New York: ACE/Macmillan, in press.

Treisman, P. U. "A Study of the Mathematics Performance of Black Students at the University of California, Berkeley." Unpublished manuscript, 1985.

U.S. Department of Education. "Faculty in Higher Education Institutions, 1988." Washington: National Center for Education Statistics, March 1990.

MARTIN J. FINKELSTEIN *is director of the New Jersey Institute for Collegiate Teaching and Learning at Seton Hall University, South Orange, New Jersey.*

MARK W. LACELLE-PETERSON *is assistant professor of education, State University of New York, Geneseo.*

In recent years senior faculty, numerically dominant among higher education's ranks, have become the focus of interest by their advocates and of derision by their critics. This chapter reviews what we know about this vital cohort and illustrates the general trends with portraits of particular subgroups.

The Senior Faculty: A Portrait and Literature Review

R. Eugene Rice, Martin J. Finkelstein

American society has always been ambivalent about professors. While education has been readily acknowledged as a fundamental building block of progressive democracy, the "egghead" has always been a focus of derision; anti-intellectualism has, historically, had a firm place as a feature of American culture. Recently, however, this ambivalence has come to focus with special intensity on a particular professional cohort: the senior faculty.

The senior faculty now in place constitutes the largest faculty cohort in the history of American higher education. This group of professors provided leadership in shaping the basic character of American colleges and universities in the second half of the twentieth century and will also play a pivotal role in selecting the faculty who will lead us into the new century. If American higher education is to be fundamentally altered over the next several years, the present cohort of senior faculty will be immensely influential in shaping the future. While the significance of this cohort of faculty is being recognized, the cohort is also being vilified by a growing stable of gadflies of the American university—the ambivalence persists.

Indeed, social scientists have been slow to focus their investigative impulse on themselves and their colleagues. Until now, the senior faculty, although numerically dominating the staffs of our colleges and universities, have remained largely unstudied as a group. The last decade, however, has seen a demonstrable increase in interest in senior faculty. Early on, that interest focused nearly exclusively on the topic of early retirement since senior faculty were defined as a blockage to new blood entering the academy. Over the past couple of years, however, the attention devoted to senior faculty has been decidedly more positive in tone, and marked by an emerging awareness

New Directions for Teaching and Learning, no. 55, Fall 1993 © Jossey-Bass Publishers

of senior faculty as a key, and largely untapped, resource for American higher education in hard economic times.

This more positive perspective on the senior faculty coincides with an increasing interest in undergraduate education and college teaching. Senior faculty, it is being acknowledged, are the ones who control the curriculum and the reward system. Senior faculty will be socializing the large new cohort of college teachers expected at the turn of the twenty-first century. Moreover, projected faculty shortages in the last years of the twentieth century suggest that in an ironic twist, America's colleges and universities may be desperately seeking to retain those seasoned faculty who in the 1980s they were seeking to push into "early" retirement.

In light of these developments and this emergent interest, this chapter seeks to identify and describe the major resources available to those who wish to learn more about senior faculty; and to summarize what we have learned about this group that is relevant to those who shape their careers and depend on their optimal performance. Additional resources are identified in Chapter Nine.

Data Sources on Senior Faculty

What we know about senior faculty comes from at least three basic sources: national surveys of higher education; general empirical studies of the American professoriate; and special empirical investigations of this group.

National Surveys. Recent national faculty surveys conducted by the National Center for Education Statistics (1990), the Carnegie Foundation for the Advancement of Teaching (1989), and the Higher Education Research Institute at the University of California, Los Angeles (Astin, Korn, and Dey, 1991) provide data on a nationally representative sample of faculty, typically disaggregated by age, rank, or tenure status. Many of the questions asked in these surveys parallel those asked on earlier national surveys, beginning in 1969 with the American Council on Education survey (Bayer, 1973). These survey data provide a useful basis for comparing the current cohort of senior faculty with past cohorts.

General Empirical Studies. These include comprehensive national studies of the American professoriate as exemplified in Bowen and Schuster (1986) and Clark (1987). Also included in this group are more focused studies such as Burke's (1988) replication of the classic Caplow and McGee (1958) study of hiring practices and Baldwin and Blackburn's (1981) application of developmental theory to academic careers (see also Baldwin, 1990).

Special Studies. Over the past few years a number of special studies have focused explicitly on senior faculty. Perhaps the largest group of these have explored faculty orientation toward retirement, especially early retirement programs (for example, Heim, 1991). Others have focused on the effects of the faculty "aging" (Lawrence and Blackburn, 1986b) and the performance

concomitants of tenure (Blackburn, 1971). A particularly instructive recent strain have been studies of faculty vitality that compare the work and career experiences of senior faculty who have achieved demonstrable success in their careers (both disciplinary and organizational) and those who have not (Clark and Corcoran, 1985; Boice, 1991; Bieber, Lawrence, and Blackburn, 1992), and also including studies of faculty burnout and career disillusionment (Boice, this volume). Many of these studies are single-institution studies; and only one explicitly compares senior faculty with their junior colleagues (Boice, 1991).

Taken together, these three basic sources illuminate three sets of questions: (1) who are the senior faculty? (2) what are their careers like? and (3) what is the nature of their work experience?

Who Are the Senior Faculty?

Before addressing these three questions in relation to the current population, we need to consider the problem of delimiting the referent of the term *senior faculty*. Unlike an original research study in which we can control the selection of a sample from a defined population, we are faced here with a wide range of definitions across our various data sources. Among the national surveys, senior faculty are defined, in fact, by age (Carnegie Foundation, 1989), rank, or tenure status (National Center for Education Statistics, 1990), usually in tandem with type of appointment (for example, full time).

The most traditional definition of senior faculty is an organizational one; that is, those faculty who have achieved seniority in the employing institution as defined by tenure and the rank of associate (at least) and preferably full professor. Such a definition says nothing about *seniority* in one's discipline, in the sense of *scholarly distinction*, which may be highly independent of organizational seniority—particularly given the current academic job market. It also says nothing about *longevity* in an academic career or even at the employing institution. In the burgeoning professional fields as opposed to liberal arts, distinguished practitioners may be appointed by colleges and universities to senior, tenured ranks. Nor, finally, does the traditional definition say anything conclusively about *age*: full professors coming from business or industry may be significantly younger than female arts and science professors who return to academe following childrearing.

Nonetheless, it is typically assumed that senior faculty are not only organizationally senior, but chronologically older and more seasoned in terms of length of service. Indeed, a significant definition of seniority is a generational one first proposed by Shirley Clark and Mary Corcoran (1985) in their pioneering work on faculty vitality. That definition identifies several successive cohorts of senior faculty of varying sizes, defined by the time at which they were first appointed to full-time academic positions—reflecting the historical moment when most came of collegiate age and attended graduate school.

The size of each such cohort would depend, of course, on the relative growth of higher education during that period as reflected in the number of hires.

This diversity in definition suggests that several distinctive subgroups of senior faculty are treated and discussed across the literature. At this juncture, except for a few select subsamples (for example, Rice, 1980), there is insufficient subgroup-specific data to allow precise comparative intergroup analysis. Thus, we use the term *senior faculty* to refer to an imprecisely defined group of tenured, full-time arts and science faculty at the rank of associate or full professor, including many who are relatively older and who have devoted relatively long periods in service to higher education (if not to their institution). We can speak of a generation of senior faculty composed of two cohorts: one in the middle of their academic careers and the other in their later stages.

In light of these definitional ambiguities, what can we say about the character of the current crop of senior faculty? First, this group includes a disproportionately large academic generation that completed their graduate education in the 1960s and the early 1970s and were absorbed into the professoriate during that period (1965–74) of higher education's explosive twentieth-century growth. This large cohort, the largest senior cohort by far in the post–World War II period, is generally characterized along a few key dimensions. First, it is relatively more homogeneous than currently entering faculty cohorts in terms of academic and socioeconomic backgrounds as well as gender. It is disproportionately white and male, from middle- and upper-middle-class backgrounds—although it is the first academic generation to reflect the wave of post–World War II democratization of the academic professions.

Second, members of this generation tended to drift into academic life at a relatively young age (frequently in their twenties) during a period of expansion and optimism (Finkelstein, 1984). They generally held high expectations for their careers in terms of opportunity and attainments. Their educational socialization was also shaped largely by meritocratic ideals of mass higher education rather than the value-added notions of universal access (Trow, 1973; Ladd and Lipset, 1975). As a cohort, this generation disproportionately overrepresents arts and science faculty who in the 1960s still dominated American higher education's faculty ranks. Furthermore, as a cohort, they have lived through a significant downturn in the industry that has crushed individual as well as generational expectations and has questioned traditional academic values.

These basic demographic characteristics find concrete expression in Rice's (1980) study of Danforth Fellows. In the mid-1970s a group of Danforth Graduate Fellowship recipients reported in detail on their own development while in early or midcareer. Since 1951 the Danforth Fellowship has been one of the major academic honors available to persons interested in preparing for a faculty career. The fellows in the study received their first ap-

pointments in the 1960s or early 1970s and now are firmly established as senior faculty. Daniel Levinson, who was to give major impetus to the study of the psychosocial development of adults, played a key role in the design of the study. His early research report, "The Psychosocial Development of Men in Early Adulthood and the Mid-Life Transition" (1978), was sent to all participating fellows along with the statements they had written while they were seniors in college regarding their career aspirations and a request for an assessment of their own personal and professional development over the intervening years.

The male faculty in the Danforth study divided into two distinct groups, typical of senior faculty today. The older group—those who began their teaching in the early 1960s—realized their professional aspirations with surprising ease. Their career patterns unfolded "on time" and in the expected progression, for example, completion of advanced degrees, first teaching appointment in accord with expectations, tenure in due course, and appropriate promotions. They had entered the academic profession at a very propitious time: new programs were being developed, funds were available for expansion, higher education was in its heyday. Speaking for others in the early group of Danforth Fellows, one faculty member candidly acknowledged, "Status in academic positions in recent years is far more a matter of where one was able to situate himself in the mid-60s than any matter of ability" (quoted in Rice, 1980, p. 4).

The second group of Danforth Fellows, those who began their professional careers in the late 1960s and early 1970s and who are now senior faculty, had a very different experience. They entered graduate school with the conviction that talented people with imagination and perseverance could substantially influence established institutions. They were also confident that higher education—the teaching profession in particular—would play a key role in effecting institutional and societal change. That confidence was seriously eroded early on, however, and replaced by substantial disillusionment, if not bitterness. The retrenchment in higher education that was much more than economic and well underway by 1974, took its toll. As one representative of this group put it, "My deluded impression was that my own passionate interests would somehow remake my social and professional environment, with its rigid demands" (quoted in Rice, 1980, p. 5). Along with many beginning their academic careers in the early 1970s, the respondent found that "[t]he available world is just too tough for that, its patterns too well entrenched. Confronted with this dismaying discovery, I have taken comfort in the fact that most of my admired and respected friends have discovered the same—or very similar—things. I have also had to give considerable thought to strategies of professional survival. A great deal of my energy has been absorbed with the questions of how to make a career I can myself respect" (quoted in Rice, 1980, p. 5).

One final demographic matter concerns family situation. This generation

tends to be one that generally reflects the experience of their age counterparts in American society in the 1990s—caught at home between the pressures of caring for aged parents and caring for children in high school and/or in college. While their "at-home" pressures may be more subtle than those of their junior colleagues, they can also be just as great.

Careers of Senior Faculty

Nearly all of the senior faculty are, by definition, tenured; and that tenured status typically brings with it a number of concomitants in the current higher education context. First, it means that senior faculty have achieved relative security and permanence both in their chosen career and in their institutional position. Virtually all are intending to complete their careers in academe and only 20 percent expect to leave their current jobs soon (National Center for Education Statistics, 1990). That reflects the severely diminished opportunities for interinstitutional mobility that have characterized the academic job market since the late 1970s (Bowen and Schuster, 1986; Burke, 1988).

If senior faculty are relatively secure in their career choice and their job, they have also typically plateaued organizationally in terms of their intra-institutional mobility. Most of those who are going to have already achieved the rank of full professor; those who have not within the usual time frame are likely going to be stuck at the associate professor rank. While some will have moved into administration—either part-time or temporarily full-time—such opportunities are limited for the vast majority of senior faculty (Kanter, 1979; Bieber, Lawrence, and Blackburn, 1992).

Most senior faculty, then, have "settled in"—in terms of career, organizational position, and job responsibilities—until retirement, which may be coming a bit later, especially at research universities (Heim, 1991)—if midsixties is still the rule (Lozier and Dooris, 1990). Typically, this "settling in" occurs just at that time when both their own interests are evolving developmentally, when their institutions are changing dramatically in their expectations of their instructional staffs, and when their disciplines may have been undergoing fundamental paradigmatic shifts. Baldwin and Blackburn (1981) have reported a gradual turning away of faculty career interests from research within their disciplines toward more interest in teaching, working with students, and in improving the life of the institution.

For many senior faculty, this change has coincided with two developments at their institution: a trend among many four-year colleges and regional universities, first noted a generation ago by Parsons and Platt (1968) and more recently by Russel Edgerton (1989), to ape the research university model that valorizes research, publication, and grants acquisition and devalues teaching and institutional citizenship. Many senior faculty are indeed currently "caught" by a change in the institutional rules whereby their talents and contributions, once prized, are now overlooked—even at the research

universities (Bieber, Lawrence, and Blackburn, 1992). This painful change is accentuated by the very different priorities of the cohort of new and junior faculty appointed over the past decade—and the rewards that accrue to them.

A second related development is, of course, the radical changes occurring in the student body in terms of race/ethnicity, age, and gender (Levine and Associates, 1989). Senior faculty are also encountering students in their classes with very different learning styles, with very serious academic skill deficiencies, and with very wide variation in prior academic preparation. Teaching strategies and practices (for example, the straight lecture) honed in the past may no longer achieve desired results. That means that even in those areas of their historic strength and emerging interest, senior faculty are being challenged in a fundamental way—frequently, as we shall learn, with limited institutional support. Finally, if institutional sands are experienced as shifting, senior faculty may turn to their academic disciplines—but find frustration there as well. A large number of the academic disciplines have, over the past generation, experienced significant paradigmatic shifts. Thus, in English or other language fields, the dominance of literary and cultural history approaches has been ceded to structuralism and deconstructionism; in biology, molecular physics has supplanted botany and zoology; in political science and sociology, quantitative empirical approaches have largely supplanted macrotheoretical and historical ones. Increasingly, senior faculty may find themselves "out of step" with the currents of theory in their own fields, and they may feel a genuine loss in their professional identification.

Work Experience of Senior Faculty

Senior faculty perceive themselves as working long and hard, at least forty-eight hours per week, in discharging their institutional responsibilities—a figure clearly comparable to the overall institutional commitments of their junior colleagues (National Center for Education Statistics, 1990). Moreover, the evidence from the university sector, at least, suggests that their work spills over into leisure pursuits and family life (Sorcinelli and Near, 1989), and becomes an essential source of life satisfaction (Finkelstein, 1984). The negative implications of that spillover for relationships with spouses and children are only too apparent.

That many observers of higher education today are skeptical of these self-reports of how hard senior faculty work is attributable to two factors. First, and this must be recognized, a small, although not insignificant, minority on many of our campuses (including research universities), variously estimated at 10–20 percent, have effectively disengaged themselves from their institutional responsibilities. These devitalized senior faculty, suffering from various forms of temporary burnout or midcareer disillusionment, need to be recognized as such—and the sources of their disaffection and estrangement addressed (see Boice, this volume).

Second, however much time senior faculty may actually devote to their institutional responsibilities, especially vis-à-vis their junior colleagues, they work differently—and that difference may affect our perceptions of them. Senior faculty typically spend less time on research leading to publication and in the preparation of research grants (although research productivity typically experiences a second peak near retirement [see Finkelstein, 1984]) and concomitantly more time in institutional governance and administrative work. They typically are more interested in teaching although they spend no more time at it (National Center for Education Statistics, 1990).

These shifts in responsibility tend to be matters of degree rather than matters of kind. The basic responsibilities of their jobs tend to remain fairly stable over the years—with variations only at the margins. Moreover, in the posttenure years, the typical mechanisms for feedback and accountability (promotion and tenure reviews) have all but dried up. While some institutions have developed arrangements for periodic posttenure review and/or growth contracting (Licata, 1986), some of the available evidence to date suggests that such arrangements tend to be fraught with ambivalence and are often seen as threats to tenure. Farmer's chapter in this volume and the experience of others, however, suggest that, over the long term, posttenure review can serve not only as a check on the quality of the work being done but, more important, as an effective stimulus for ongoing renewal and professional growth. The autonomy of senior faculty often cuts them off from constructive feedback. Also, the institutional recognition of quality teaching and other accomplishments is all too infrequent an occurrence in the lives of tenured faculty.

The emerging evidence suggests, first, that these mid- and late-career adjustments tend to be shaped (that is, they are foreseeable) early on during the career's first decade (see Boice, this volume), and, second, that vitality seems to be associated with the availability of opportunities subject not only to individual motivation but very much to organizational brokering and entrepreneurship (see LaCelle-Peterson and Finkelstein, this volume). These findings suggest that how faculty adjust to their work experience in mid- and later career are both predictable *and* subject to organizational intervention.

Having said all of this, the literature is equally clear in its testament to the relatively high level of job satisfaction among senior faculty as a group. Every major national survey reports levels of job satisfaction at the 80 percent level or higher, including satisfaction with their institution, their career, and their job (although not necessarily their salary) (Carnegie Foundation, 1989; National Center for Education Statistics, 1990; Astin, Korn, and Dey, 1991). This satisfaction is no doubt a matter of "settling for" what one learns is realistic as one moves on from midlife. In part, this also no doubt represents a perception on the part of American academics of the real opportunity that academic life does offer for the autonomous pursuit of one's interests.

However, to return to the experiences of the Danforth Fellows, one

theme that stands out is their disappointment in the lack of colleagueship, "the paucity of professional dialogue." Viewed from the outside, the life of the professor seems particularly rich in opportunities for sophisticated intellectual exchange and enlivening participation in a community of scholars. This is clearly not what most find. As one of the fellows who is now a senior faculty member put it, "I am increasingly aware of the deadening effect of the faculty, a group at least as political as intellectual, indeed, a group that is even anti-intellectual precisely because it holds so tightly to its own narrow intellectual orientation" (quoted in Rice, 1980, p. 4).

As today's senior faculty are joined, or prepare to be joined over the next decade, by a substantial new cohort of junior colleagues, the prospect of finding the colleagueship they have long sought in intergenerational relationships with a new academic generation remains a tantalizing possibility. While a number of senior-junior "mentoring" initiatives are indeed already underway, first impressions suggest that to date senior faculty have not seen in their junior colleagues such an opportunity (nor have their junior colleagues seen it in them).

Implications and Unanswered Questions

Taken together what do the research findings here suggest about what we know and what we need to do? First, they suggest that within the senior faculty, there are diversities—generational as well as disciplinary—that need to be taken into account for testing and elucidation.

Second, having recognized the diversities, there are nonetheless overriding commonalities that are rooted primarily in career stage, and associated changes in interests and institutional involvement, and in the academic generation in which this faculty cohort came of age, that set them apart in terms both of their needs and interests from their more junior colleagues—and indeed from the next generation of faculty who are now in graduate school.

If senior faculty are at a distinctive career stage and hale from a dominant academic generation, these distinctions are reflected in a greater interest in teaching and in the lives of their institution. On the face of it, this augurs well for American higher education. Indeed, the data suggest that in their number and in their experience and interests, the senior faculty constitute a resource, heretofore largely unacknowledged and untapped, for the renewal of undergraduate education in the last decade of the twentieth century and beyond.

Teaching can take on a new meaning during the senior years of the professoriate. Much has been made of the changing role of the mentor in the second half of life. Levinson (1978) and others have argued that as a part of the midlife transition, people shift from having mentors to taking on the role themselves, from having a mentor to being one. Faculty are in a particularly advantageous place to take advantage of this developmental change. Relationships with students have the potential for becoming even more

rewarding than earlier in the faculty career. This is particularly true in terms of potential relationships between faculty members and the growing number of older, nontraditional students. Adult learners have a maturing respect for experience-based knowledge; they also have a special appreciation for the capacity to place what is being taught in a broader context and a larger perspective. The difficulty here, however, is that many of our nontraditional programs are recent additions introduced after most of the present senior faculty were firmly established in traditional settings. Organizational flexibility and the capability to move laterally in institutions are needed if these potentially more rewarding teaching opportunities are to be made more readily available to senior faculty.

The Carnegie Foundation's special report entitled *Campus Life: In Search of Community* (1990) highlights the gulf that has developed between students and faculty on most campuses. The report refers to separate student and faculty cultures. If senior faculty are going to benefit from and contribute to a renewed emphasis on undergraduate teaching, that separation is going to have to be transcended.

Developmentally, there are two transition periods among senior faculty that might well require special attention. First, the midlife transition about which so much has been written continues to be a significant factor among the younger group of senior faculty (those in their midforties who were powerfully influenced by the turbulent 1960s). These faculty continually press for greater diversity and broader inclusion in colleges and universities and are struggling to relate their own idealism to the realities of institutions in recession. The second transition period with which faculty are now grappling—one that has gone largely unnoticed—is being confronted by professors in their midfifties. These faculty, who were undergraduates in the 1950s, have had permanent positions, often in the same institution, and are beginning to ask if what they have experienced professionally is all there is to life. Also, despite good health and personal vigor, they are beginning to anticipate retirement careers, or are entertaining thoughts of one last move before retirement. This transition is not receiving the attention it deserves. Maintaining the vitality of our most senior faculty is critical if, as is being suggested here, they have a key role to play in shaping the future of American higher education.

Throughout this review, references have been made to the importance of providing new organizational opportunities for senior faculty in the form of institutional interventions that might promote renewed growth and change. Two problems are endemic to such efforts. First, the career ladder of the professor has, typically, only three rungs; many faculty are tenured, full professors at the age of forty, with no place left to go. There is no opportunity structure available to them; they are, in Kanter's (1979, pp. 3–9) term, "stuck." The second major problem with the professorial career is the im-

plicit assumption that the way one moves ahead or advances professionally is to narrow further or accentuate one's specialization.

The challenge here is one of organizational development. Senior faculty, especially, need multifaceted organizational structures that will encourage them to broaden their horizons, approach their work in different and imaginative ways, and find new opportunities to grow and change. The research of E. H. Schein (1978) on "career anchors" and M. J. Driver (1979, 1982) on "career concept types," although focused primarily on managerial careers, argues convincingly that there are different orientations to work or careers that need to be accommodated in organizational settings. This research suggests that heterogeneity rather than homogeneity should be valued, and that individuals should be encouraged to build on their strengths and to pursue their shifting interests and commitments. In a dynamic organizational setting, where new opportunities and options are made readily available, senior faculty can continue to thrive personally and professionally, while serving the changing needs of the institutions, which is precisely what, as the literature points out, they want to do.

Especially promising for senior faculty is the effort, urged on by the Carnegie Foundation's recent report *Scholarship Reconsidered* (Boyer, 1990), to broaden the conception of what counts as scholarly work. This effort, which is receiving widespread attention, has the potential for providing a wider range of legitimate scholarly options. Included here is not only greater appreciation for scholarly aspects of undergraduate teaching, but a new emphasis on professional service and the kind of integrative scholarship to which senior faculty, with their seasoned wisdom and experience, are best prepared to contribute (Rice, 1991). The remainder of the chapters in this volume constitute a set of initial efforts to realize the multifaceted promise of senior faculty careers.

References

Astin, A. W., Korn, W., and Dey, E. "The American College Teacher: National Norms for the 1989–90 HERI Faculty Survey." Los Angeles: Higher Education Research Institute, University of California, 1991.

Baldwin, R. G. "Faculty Career Stages and Implications for Professional Development." In J. H. Shuster, D. W. Wheeler, and Associates (eds.), *Enhancing Faculty Careers: Strategies for Development and Renewal.* San Francisco: Jossey-Bass, 1990.

Baldwin, R. G., and Blackburn, R. T. "The Academic Career as a Developmental Process: Implications for Higher Education." *Journal of Higher Education,* 1981, 52 (6), 598–614.

Bayer, A. E. *Teaching Faculty in Academe: 1972–73.* American Council on Education Research Reports, vol. 8, no. 2. Washington, D.C.: American Council on Education, 1973.

Bieber, J. P., Lawrence, J. H., and Blackburn, R. T. "Through the Years: Faculty and Their Changing Institution." *Change,* 1992, 24 (4), 28–35.

Blackburn, R. T. *The Professor's Role in a Changing Society.* ERIC Research Reports, no. 10. Washington, D.C.: ERIC Clearinghouse on Higher Education, 1971.

Boice, R. "New Faculty as Teachers." *Journal of Higher Education,* 1991, 62 (2), 150–173.

Bowen, H. R., and Schuster, J. H. *American Professors: A National Resource Imperiled.* New York: Oxford University Press, 1986.

Boyer, E. *Scholarship Reconsidered: Priorities for the Professoriate.* Princeton, N.J.: Carnegie Foundation for the Advancement of Teaching, 1990.

Burke, D. *A New Academic Marketplace.* Westport, Conn.: Greenwood Press, 1988.

Caplow, T., and McGee, R. J. *The Academic Marketplace.* New York: Basic Books, 1958.

Carnegie Foundation for the Advancement of Teaching. *The Condition of the Professoriate: Attitudes and Trends, 1989.* Princeton, N.J.: Carnegie Foundation for the Advancement of Teaching, 1989.

Carnegie Foundation for the Advancement of Teaching. *Campus Life: In Search of Community: A Special Report.* Princeton, N.J.: Princeton University Press, 1990.

Clark, B. *The Academic Life: Small Worlds, Different Worlds.* Princeton, N.J.: Carnegie Foundation for the Advancement of Teaching, 1987.

Clark, S., and Corcoran, M. "Individual and Organizational Contributions to Faculty Vitality." In S. Clark and D. R. Lewis (eds.), *Faculty Vitality and Institutional Productivity: Critical Perspectives for Higher Education.* New York: Teacher College Press, Columbia University, 1985.

Driver, M. J. "Career Concept and Career Management in Organizations." In C. L. Cooper (ed.), *Behavior Problems in Organizations.* Englewood Cliffs, N.J.: Prentice-Hall, 1979.

Driver, M. J. "Career Concepts: A New Approach to Career Research." In R. Katz (ed.), *Career Issues in Human Resource Management.* Englewood Cliffs, N.J.: Prentice-Hall, 1982.

Edgerton, R. "The Next Academic Revolution: David Riesman on the Next Generation of the Professoriate." *American Association for Higher Education Bulletin,* 1989, *42* (1), 4–8.

Finkelstein, M. J. *The American Academic Profession.* Columbus: Ohio State University Press, 1984.

Heim, P. "The NACUB/TIAA-CREF Survey of College and University Retirees." *Research Dialogues,* Oct. 1991, no. 31.

Kanter, R. M. "Changing the Shape of Work: Reform in Academe." In *Current Issues in Higher Education,* no. 1. Washington, D.C.: American Association for Higher Education, 1979.

Ladd, E. C., and Lipset, S. M. *The Divided Academy.* New York: McGraw-Hill, 1975.

Lawrence, J. H., and Blackburn, R. T. "Aging and Faculty Distribution of Their Work Effort." Paper presented at the annual meeting of the Association for the Study of Higher Education, San Antonio, Tex., Feb. 20–23, 1986a. (ED 268903)

Lawrence, J. H., and Blackburn, R. T. "Aging and the Quality of Faculty Job Performance." *Review of Educational Research,* 1986b, *56* (3), 265–290.

Levine, A., and Associates. *Shaping Higher Education's Future: Demographic Realities and Opportunities, 1990–2000.* San Francisco: Jossey-Bass, 1989.

Levinson, D. C. "The Psychosocial Development of Men in Early Adulthood and Mid-Life Transition." In D. C. Levinson, C. Darrow, E. Klein, M. Levinson, and B. McKee, *The Seasons of a Man's Life.* New York: Knopf, 1978.

Licata, C. M. *Post-Tenure Faculty Evaluation: Threat or Opportunity?* ASHE-ERIC Higher Education Research Report, no. 1. Washington, D.C.: ASHE-ERIC Higher Education Reports, George Washington University, 1986.

Lozier, O. G., and Dooris, M. S. *Faculty Retirement Projections Beyond 1994: Effects of Policy on Individual Choice.* Boulder, Colo.: Western Interstate Commission for Higher Education, 1990.

Melendez, W. A., and Guzman, R. M. *Burnout: The New Academic Disease.* ASHE-ERIC Higher Education Research Report, no. 9. Washington, D.C.: ASHE-ERIC Higher Education Reports, George Washington University, 1983.

National Center for Education Statistics. *Faculty in Higher Education Institutions, 1988.* Report of the 1988 National Survey of Postsecondary Faculty (NSOPF-88). Washington, D.C.: Office of Educational Research and Improvement, U.S. Department of Education, 1990.

Parsons, T., and Platt, G. M. *The American Academic Profession: A Pilot Study.* Cambridge, Mass.: Harvard University Press, 1968.

Rice, R. E. "Dreams and Actualities: Danforth Fellows in Mid-Career." *American Association for Higher Education Bulletin,* 1980, *32* (8), 3–16.

Rice, R. E. "The New American Scholar: Scholarship and the Purposes of the University." *Metropolitan Universities: An International Journal,* 1991, *1* (4), 7–18.

Schein, E. H. *Career Dynamics: Matching Individual and Organizational Needs.* Reading, Mass.: Addison-Wesley, 1978.

Sorcinelli, M. D., and Near, J. "Relations Between Work and Life Away from Work Among University Faculty." *Journal of Higher Education,* 1989, *60* (1), 59–81.

Trow, M. "The Transition from Elite to Mass to Universal Access in Higher Education." Paper presented at meeting of the Organization for Economic Cooperation and Development, Paris, 1973.

R. EUGENE RICE is dean of the faculty at Antioch College, Yellow Springs, Ohio.

MARTIN J. FINKELSTEIN is director of the New Jersey Institute for Collegiate Teaching and Learning at Seton Hall University, South Orange, New Jersey.

*Institutional support is a key to sustaining the vitality of higher
education's most experienced teachers. Research on eleven campuses
shows that institutions need to create collaborative teaching structures
and to broker significant opportunities for individual growth.*

Institutions Matter: Campus Teaching Environments' Impact on Senior Faculty

Mark W. LaCelle-Peterson, Martin J. Finkelstein

Senior faculty members' individual and collective engagement in teaching is
vital to both the immediate and the long-term future of higher education in
the United States. Today, tenured associate and full professors, directly or
through their oversight of adjunct faculty and graduate students, bear the
lion's share of responsibility for college teaching. In addition, because they
select and socialize the new faculty who will eventually replace them, they
are building the foundation for college teaching in the next century. Clearly,
higher education's present and future success as a teaching enterprise depends on the senior faculty. What is all too frequently overlooked, however,
is the crucial corollary: *senior faculty members' success as teachers depends on
the support of their institutions.* Too often observers assume that senior faculty,
securely tenured and with years of teaching experience under their belts, are
impervious to circumstance. Their styles and levels of success as teachers
were presumably set in graduate school or during their first academic appointment, and any variations in enthusiasm or skill they display as teachers
are simply evidence of inherent individual differences, neither the result of,
nor amenable to, institutional policies.

Contrary to this common wisdom, the findings of a study of 111 senior
faculty members on eleven New Jersey campuses show that teaching vitality
is, at least in part, a product of a positive teaching climate: one that affords

The research reported here was supported by a grant from the Pew Charitable Trusts to the
New Jersey Institute for Collegiate Teaching and Learning at Seton Hall University.

professors opportunities to work together on teaching and to experience professional growth as teacher-scholars within their disciplines. The study sought to answer three questions: First, how do senior faculty members as individuals experience teaching? Do they remain engaged in teaching after years in the classroom? Why or why not? Second, how do institutions enhance or diminish the teaching experience for senior faculty? Do institutional policies or characteristics matter in relation to faculty members' individual or collective "teaching engagement?" Third, given the answers to the first two questions, can institutions and their senior faculty, working together, do more to create institutional climates that support vital, engaged teaching for all faculty members?

A two-year action research project shaped by these questions is described in five sections below. The first section presents the origins of the project, the questions that drove it, and the process set up to answer them. The second section presents what we learned from senior faculty about the role of institutions in supporting them as teachers. The final two sections outline the wider policy implications of these findings.

Eleven-Campus Study

The desire to explore these questions grew out of the realization that the faculty side of the demographic equation sketched in Chapter One of this volume held true for the state of New Jersey. A study of faculty demographics revealed that, in the short run, senior faculty were, and would remain, the dominant cohort in all sectors of higher education (Finkelstein, 1988). In the long run, however, once the faculty cohort hired between 1965 and 1973 begin to retire, a tremendous turnover can be expected. In both the short and the long term, senior faculty are clearly the key to the quality and effectiveness of college and university teaching.

In light of these demographic realities, and inspired by the great success of its Partners in Learning Program in engaging faculty on very different kinds of campuses—senior faculty in particular—in reflection-based teaching innovation (see Smith and Smith, this volume), the New Jersey Institute for Collegiate Teaching and Learning conceptualized an action research project to explore the role of institutional support in sustaining the development of senior faculty as teachers, and to encourage greater institutional efforts to create and/or maintain positive teaching climates. Eventually, eleven campuses—public and private, two-year, four-year, and university—agreed to participate (see Table 2.1).

Two groups—a "campus advisory board" composed of the chief academic officers from the eleven campuses and a "research advisory board" made up of recognized scholars on faculty in higher education—guided the project. Separate discussions with each advisory group began with two questions: how should we define "senior faculty"? and whom within the defined

Table 2.1. Participating Campuses by Type

	Public	Private	Total
Two-year	3	—	3
Four-year	1	4	5
University	2	1	3
Total	6	5	11

group ought we to interview? In answer to the first question, a general demographic definition emerged in both groups: senior faculty were those tenured individuals who had taught full time in colleges or universities for at least fifteen years; these faculty members were typically forty-five years of age or older, and could look forward to as many as twenty more years of teaching. In considering the second question—how to sample this large and diverse group—discussion centered on two characteristics of faculty: their degree of engagement in teaching, and their degree of influence among colleagues. These characteristics defined, on the basis of administrators' perceptions (not empirical evidence), three potentially overlapping subgroups of senior faculty who could provide important perspectives on the research questions. Those recognized by faculty colleagues and administrators as exceptionally engaged in teaching could provide "best case" exemplars to guide and inspire. Those faculty seen as exceptionally disengaged teachers, on the other hand, were of particular interest to administrators alarmed at the student complaints they provoked. Given the action orientation of the project, the insights of a third group, faculty "opinion leaders" who helped shape the campus environment, would contribute to a clearer understanding of how teaching was valued and could be enhanced.

In the end, twelve senior faculty members were nominated from each campus; each list included professors from a wide range of disciplines as well as some who were perceived to exhibit different degrees of influence and engagement. Though these categories played no role in the subsequent research or analysis, their use ensured that a wide variety of views would be expressed. From eight to twelve professors on each campus agreed to participate in one- to two-hour structured interviews. Table 2.2 presents gender and disciplinary distributions of those interviewed.

The interviews themselves consisted of fifty open-ended questions focused on two areas: teaching experience and teaching environment. The former included questions about respondents' early teaching experiences, how the teaching of a particular course had changed over the years, the kinds of assignments they gave students, and how they maintained interest in frequently taught courses. The latter included questions about changes in students over the years, how colleagues in and outside the department influenced their teaching, the role of formal faculty development programs, and institutional promotion and tenure policies. The sample was not drawn

Table 2.2. Faculty Participants by Gender and Discipline

Discipline	Men	Women	Total
Anthropology	1	—	1
Architecture	—	1	1
Art	2	—	2
Art history	1	—	1
Biology	7	1	8
Business education	—	2	2
Chemistry	5	1	6
Community health	1	—	1
Comparative literature	—	1	1
Computer science	1	—	1
Ecology	1	—	1
Economics	7	2	9
Education	—	2	2
Engineering	7	—	7
English	10	8	18
History	5	—	5
Humanities	1	—	1
Languages	1	4	5
Management	5	—	5
Mathematics	4	3	7
Nursing	—	5	5
Philosophy	2	1	3
Physics	4	—	4
Political science	—	1	1
Psychology	5	3	8
Religion	2	—	2
Sociology	3	—	3
Theater	1	—	1
Total	76	35	111

randomly, nor did each interview cover all possible questions; as in Clark's (1987) study of academic life, the conversations followed the individual respondents' interests and circumstances.

What We Found

Analysis of the interviews yielded three major findings, elaborated in the following sections. First, senior faculty members care a great deal about teaching and experience it as fulfilling. Second, however, in the normal course of "business as usual," they typically find little opportunity—formally or informally—to focus on teaching. Teaching is isolated, and poorer for that isolation. Without periodic opportunities to revitalize their professional lives generally and their teaching lives in particular, faculty members report that their "teaching vitality" tends to slip. Third, two ways emerged in which institutions support and enhance faculty development as teachers: *creating*

structural alterations in the teaching situation to eliminate the isolation of teaching, and *brokering individual opportunities* to revitalize individual professors.

Senior Faculty Enjoy Teaching. The first question considered was "How do senior faculty members as individuals experience teaching?" Since many had taught hundreds of courses and thousands of students, did these campus veterans still find joy in teaching? The data were clear: *the overwhelming majority enjoy teaching and care a great deal about student learning.* Though a number expressed greater and lesser degrees of dissatisfaction about students' level of academic preparation in recent years, and though those whose teaching assignments were repetitive noted the difficulty this posed, senior faculty members cared a great deal about teaching. Not only did most express a strong commitment to their roles as teachers, many answered the question "What keeps you fresh as a teacher?" with the emphatic reply, "The students!"

While faculty members generally reported a positive attitude toward teaching, some reported relatively more frequent innovation and revision in their teaching than did others. Some, in fact, reported that the repetition that characterized their teaching assignments was wearying—though the occasional spark of interest by a student made it worthwhile. A few individual faculty members reported great variations in teaching vitality across their own careers. These faculty, whom we have called "turn arounds," reported periods in their careers during which they "burned out" on teaching or on their institution as a whole. They did not, however, remain in this state, but instead eventually found renewed vitality. In analyzing what all of the senior faculty told us about their teaching experiences and the "milestones" in their teaching careers, we found that, to greater and lesser degrees, such swings in teaching vitality were common to many faculty careers—and that the swings "up" were often mediated by an institutional variable, a point to be elaborated below.

In the big picture, the data suggest that while professors are highly motivated as individuals by the intrinsic rewards of teaching—interaction with students and material or "performance" (as clearly illustrated by faculty members who reported "getting energy" from performing well in front of a roomful of students)—their teaching vitality cannot be sustained indefinitely without extrinsic or institutional support.

How can institutions support teaching vitality among their senior professors? In the interviews, we inquired into three vehicles that might, logically, provide such support. First, given the high level of autonomy among professors and the value placed on collegiality, we explored the role of informal collegial interactions in sustaining teaching. Second, given that the department or division is often the faculty member's most meaningful unit of membership, we asked how departmental policies and routine departmental interactions influenced faculty members' teaching. Third, as each of the

participating campuses had faculty development policies or programs in place, we asked how these supported faculty in their roles as teachers. After reporting briefly on these vehicles, we will elaborate on the two types of institutional interventions that mattered most for senior faculty.

Collegial Interaction Regarding Teaching Is Limited. Despite their individual interest in and commitment to teaching, professors report little collegial interaction around it. Half of the interviewees do not discuss teaching with their colleagues. One in five discusses teaching with his or her colleagues around the department, another one in ten talks about things related to teaching, like books, lab materials, or complaints about students, with his or her colleagues. One in ten reports discussions about teaching with colleagues across disciplines. The patterns of informal interaction around teaching reflect the fact that teaching is the very part of faculty work that is most individual and that is almost always conducted in isolation.

One additional finding: informal interaction is, in the experience of some, shaped by institutional factors. Several professors at one private campus mentioned that the disappearance of a popular faculty gathering place reduced the amount of collegial interaction—including interaction around teaching—since the informal venue for those conversations was no longer available. Respondents at two community colleges and two private institutions commented that increased use of adjuncts for teaching, and the resultant burden on the remaining fulltimers to take care of department business, left them feeling more harried with less time for conversation. Faculty at two universities noted that, even for those interested in talking about teaching, it was hard to find time and interested partners.

Departmental Discussion of Teaching Is Scarce. We also asked faculty whether they discuss teaching formally at the department level. Here, even more pronouncedly than with regard to informal conversation, they report little if any interaction around teaching. One in fourteen faculty members said that teaching was a topic of discussion in department meetings. Three-quarters of those interviewed reported no interaction around classroom teaching in department meetings; one-quarter said that occasional discussions of curriculum revision were the only teaching-related agenda items. In all cases, informational and business matters dominated departmental agendas. As one reflective faculty member characterized it, "We talk a lot about the prerequisites to teaching, but not about teaching itself." To many, the status quo was quite acceptable. Several went so far as to express satisfaction that the department was not "intrusive" in regard to teaching—being left alone to do one's own thing was the best some faculty members could wish from their departments. In some cases, faculty members opined that keeping teaching off the agenda was just as well because their departmental colleagues had been together for too long to learn from each other about teaching: each had a position to reiterate, and the arguments were worn and predictable.

Though departments generally turned out to be the missing player in interaction around teaching, there were important exceptions. Nursing departments in particular structured their teaching work collaboratively and provided for significant interaction around teaching, both formally and informally. Natural science departments likewise, in a more limited way, found a common focus for teaching interaction in their laboratory experiences. In addition, faculty members in one English department reported frequent interaction around classroom teaching issues; this was carried on outside official departmental channels, however. Most faculty members who wanted to focus on teaching together with their colleagues, however, did so through institution-wide faculty development programs—not through departmental structures.

Faculty Development Programs Attracted Many. Some faculty members reported significant interaction around teaching in other institution-wide programs. Each of the eleven participating campuses was home to at least one, in most cases two or three, ongoing faculty development programs (such as the Partners in Learning program, a Writing Across the Curriculum program, or a Race, Class, and Gender (Multicultural) faculty seminar) in which faculty from across the institution participated voluntarily. In addition, each campus sponsored occasional series of teaching workshops. One in four faculty members participate (or have participated) in one or more of the ongoing programs. These programs provide a structure for reflection on teaching, and often require faculty member participants to revise a course, in terms of both content and teaching methods. Participants in these programs are self-selected; those who participate in them found them to be beneficial, and others who did not personally participate often knew them to have positive reputations. Valuable though they were to participants, many were hesitant to participate in non-discipline-based programs. Two of five faculty members interviewed had not participated in any faculty development effort; one in five had only attended occasional seminars.

What Made a Difference?

While collegial interaction and structured faculty development programs provide important sustenance for faculty interest in teaching, analysis of the mass of interview data suggests that, from the organizational perspective, two classes of opportunities provide the most meaningful structure and support for vital engagement in teaching. Near the end of the interview with each faculty member, after having discussed the issues already noted, we asked two questions that promoted reflection on what mattered over the course of their careers. The first asked what milestones or stages they had passed through as teachers; the second asked what sustained them, that is, what gave them the energy to keep going semester after semester. As already noted, to the latter question, a number of faculty responded "the students"; many also

noted their love of the discipline. But in addition to these factors faculty members talked about opportunities for collaboratively structured teaching and for significant personal growth.

Collaboration on Teaching. Teaching experiences that were reported with greatest enthusiasm and appreciation by those who were still involved, and with a great sense of loss by those whose involvement has ceased, involve collaboration on teaching marked by substantive discussion of content in connection with a common group of students. Frequently, faculty report these interactions in the context of team teaching—an arrangement that on some campuses has become less common these days due to resource constraints, but that was becoming more common on others in the form of "core course clusters" through which students fulfilled general education requirements, or as part of special honors programs or retention programs. Faculty who had taught in such course clusters at the freshman or sophomore level in which two or more faculty members collaborate in teaching a common group of students with some degree of coordination report that the experience was the occasion for their most meaningful teaching interactions.

Departments much less frequently provide a forum for teaching-embedded interaction; only nursing and, to a lesser degree, science departments commonly do. Faculty in nursing, for example, report frequent cooperative interaction both in team teaching individual courses and in constantly monitoring the real-world success of their students in clinicals and of their graduates on state nursing board examinations. The addition of these very real and externally monitored standards led to intense and focused interaction on teaching. Two nursing faculty members in separate institutions noted that, in their perception, faculty colleagues in other departments who were looking for ways to improve teaching to help their students were struggling with issues nursing departments had dealt with for years.

Limited dimensions of collaboration arose in departments that structured interaction around particular aspects of teaching. In laboratory sciences, for example, faculty report their most significant interactions with colleagues and students took place in laboratory settings. Teaching one on one or with small groups in the laboratory setting seems to many scientists to be the essence of science teaching. Faculty members' collegial teaching interactions likewise are often centered around shared laboratory space and equipment; they interacted less around the teaching of classroom sections of courses. Finally, faculty in English departments on two campuses report intensive interaction focused around departmental grading of final writing assignments from all sections of composition courses. The economics department on a third campus, and an engineering department on a fourth, framed teaching-embedded interactions by using common examinations (or at least common portions) in multiple-section courses.

Significant Brokered Opportunities. In addition to valuing structured interaction around teaching, faculty report significant benefits from oppor-

tunities to venture outside of the classroom for a time for renewal. The traditional faculty development practices of periodic sabbaticals and support for travel to scholarly or professional meetings are highly valued by faculty members. For some faculty members, spending a sabbatical semester or year in scholarship or research is literally revitalizing. For others, participation in a fellowship program that takes them off campus to interact around teaching issues with other scholars in their discipline is remembered as a significant turning point in their career. Such opportunities were particularly significant for those few faculty who were isolated as lone specialists or lone members of a discipline on their campuses (though these were not the only faculty who benefited from them). Still others noted that time spent at their own institution outside the classroom—for example, a stint as department chair or as an acting administrator—provides a break that leaves them eager to return to teaching and energized for the task.

Two points about such brokered opportunities stand out. First, their significance comes from the break in the routine, regardless of whether the professor leaves the campus. Second, faculty members typically avail themselves of these opportunities via the encouragement of their colleagues or administrators. That means that these opportunities can be "missed" in the absence of such second-party intervention. It also means that when the opportunity comes, it is experienced as an outside recognition of ability—an extrinsic reward.

What Can Campuses Do?

In light of the findings above, what can campuses do to support the continuing development of their senior professors as teachers? While no one answer fits all campuses, the patterns that emerged on the diverse group of campuses participating in the study suggest concrete strategies.

Provide a Stimulus-Rich Environment. If there is one general principle to be drawn from the data, it is that even a small faculty will benefit from having a wide variety of options available. Indeed, the two smallest institutions in terms of number of faculty had the widest array of opportunities available, the highest degree of participation in them, and the highest degree of satisfaction with the teaching situation, *even among the few who knowingly chose not to participate.* Judging from the evidence gathered on the eleven campuses, it appears that variety is important both because it provides a wider range of options for faculty members as individuals (who may find different options valuable at different points in their personal and professional development) *and* because the options seem to have a multiplier effect. The impact of the whole range of options on a given campus appears to be greater than the sum of the parts.

Provide Opportunities for Collective/Collaborative Teaching. Changes in the structure of teaching that foster collaboration allow individuals to

rethink their own teaching practice. Faculty who had experienced team teaching found it to be a revitalizing experience. Austin and Baldwin (1992) report on a range of models that support faculty collaboration around teaching, including inter- and multidisciplinary models. Their discussion underscores the point that opportunities for fostering collective interaction around teaching need not come only in the form of providing for expensive double-staffing of existing courses. Several models in which faculty teams teach multiple courses might be considered. Other institutional efforts might also present opportunities. For example, campuses that are considering changes in freshman core requirements or general education revisions might find in them a valuable opportunity for faculty growth.

The benefits that accrue include development of teaching ability, intellectual stimulation, and closer connection to the campus community (Austin and Baldwin, 1992, p. 41). In addition to benefiting students, creating community around teaching is important for faculty members themselves.

Broker Opportunities for Individuals. As important as collective engagement in teaching is for many faculty members, the individual dimension is also of vital importance. Systematic (not serendipitous) brokering of opportunities to individuals is experienced as an act of valuing the individuals' past contributions and future potential. Encouraging faculty members to apply for fellowships or awards can be a form of validation, a vote of confidence. Whether opportunities are created within the institution or are identified outside it, providing information, encouragement, and whatever support is appropriate can enhance individual vitality.

One illustrative example comes from a community college where the teaching load is heavy. This institution developed a program of "mini-sabbaticals" through which faculty received a one-course reduction in teaching load to carry out a proposed project of research or scholarship, the results of which they presented to their faculty colleagues. Though the award is relatively modest, the payoff to the individuals participating *and to their colleagues who look forward to each semester's presentations* is significant.

Such small-scale awards alone are, of course, not enough, but each additional increment probably adds significantly to the overall perception of an environment that values teaching and teachers. In order for such strategies to succeed, those in the position to broker the opportunities must know their faculty members' individual strengths and interests.

Bring the Departments into the Picture. While departments are the administrative center of teaching on most campuses, they are often not the center of faculty interaction around teaching. The data from this study provide only a few examples of departments that focus faculty energies on teaching. Those faculty members who decline to participate in campuswide, teaching-related, faculty development programs, however, often note that such generic faculty development programs are limited, and that programs related to teaching their chosen discipline would be of greater interest. At least one fac-

ulty member, a department chair at a private university, was determined to institute departmental seminars on teaching. Campuses might also look for in-house examples of departments where beneficial collaboration around teaching is already taking place for close-to-home models.

Maintain Institution-wide Faculty Development Programs. These programs are of great benefit to many faculty; they are not the answer for all. Faculty and administrators alike spoke of the limits of generic faculty development. Still, the value of these programs is in providing a forum for faculty from a range of disciplines to share a common focus and to learn from each other. While they do not meet all needs, they can have a significant impact and contribute to some sense of campuswide community.

Epilogue

Thus far, we have focused on the question of how campuses are now, or could better be, supporting their senior faculty's continuing development as teachers. But would faculty on any given campus respond to such support? One result of our conversations with these faculty suggests they would. In addition to asking about their histories as teachers and about the current state of their institutional teaching environments, we asked them to tell us what they would like to see in the "best of all worlds" in regard to teaching. While some of the answers given to the question might strike administrators as predictable and impossible to create—such as reduced course loads, particularly in community colleges, and better-prepared students—many of the answers matched the recommendations above.

Faculty said they want more of what their experiences suggest make for growth and development as teachers. For example, faculty want more intellectually oriented collegial interaction in general, and feel that it will contribute to their development as teachers. Faculty want opportunities to expand their horizons through fellowships, even in small doses such as the minisabbaticals described above, or through interinstitutional exchange, in order to bring new perspectives into the classroom. Faculty, especially those who have experienced team teaching, also want to work collectively again in teaching. Finally, many faculty members would like to see good teaching recognized and rewarded. By focusing attention on brokering opportunities for senior faculty and on creating multiple supports on campus for excellent teaching, institutions can indeed matter—for the vitality of their faculty and, ultimately, for the experience of their students.

References

Austin, A., and Baldwin, R. *Faculty Collaboration.* ASHE-ERIC Higher Education Research Report, no. 7. Washington, D.C.: ASHE-ERIC Higher Education Reports, George Washington University, 1992.

Clark, B. R. *Academic Life: Small Worlds, Different Worlds.* Princeton, N.J.: Carnegie Foundation
for the Advancement of Teaching, 1987.

Finkelstein, M. J. *Staffing New Jersey's Colleges and Universities for the 21st Century: Faculty Supply and Demand, 1987–2014.* Trenton: New Jersey Department of Higher Education, 1988.

MARK W. LACELLE-PETERSON *is assistant professor of education, State University
of New York, Geneseo.*

MARTIN J. FINKELSTEIN *is director of the New Jersey Institute for Collegiate
Teaching and Learning at Seton Hall University, South Orange, New Jersey.*

Repeated interviews with midlife professors identified as seriously disillusioned revealed that the turning points behind their career derailments fit a reliable sequence of events that typically occurred early in their careers. Programs in which disillusioned midcareer faculty have experienced renewal have focused on involving them as mentors for new faculty or as partners in contracts for change with departmental chairpeople—measures that might have helped prevent disillusionment earlier in their careers.

Primal Origins and Later Correctives for Midcareer Disillusionment

Robert Boice

Folk wisdom holds that middle age brings to each of us the face we deserve. So too for careers, some of which are happily attractive and some sadly disillusioning at their midpoints. While few of us seriously believe that angelic faces reflect faultless lives, we may accept the career notion less critically. If we dismiss the career failures of our unhappiest colleagues as deserved, we may needlessly doom others to repeat their experiences. We might also persist in doubting the value of programs in faculty development for our colleagues who have grown disenchanted and disengaged by midcareer.

The premise I begin with here is that careers gone awry merit patient inquiries into their turning points. Such an inquiry could include, as I do here, a deeper appreciation of the costs of ignoring the problem of disillusioned faculty at midcareer. And it might address the matter of whether the most entrenched of unproductive and oppositional colleagues can be redirected to happier careers and faces. Notions about the hopelessness of "deadwood" make up a significantly misleading part of academic folklore.

Three Study Questions

When, over two decades ago, I decided to build programs for reengaging disillusioned midcareer faculty, I met with considerable skepticism. (I still do.) Not only did administrators and faculty development practitioners doubt that long-disengaged colleagues could be revived, the individuals best able to help also wondered about the need. Some of the higher administrators in a position to fund and authorize my efforts wondered about the commonality

of the problem. Perhaps, they supposed, the significant cases comprised no more than a handful of midcareer faculty per campus. Moreover, they added, fewer still were likely a bother. Why not, I was asked, leave these unfortunate but exceptional cases to further vegetate or petrify, and move on to other areas of faculty development?

The near self-righteousness in these reservations, none of it visibly based on facts, inspired me to conduct systematic inquiries.

Question 1: How common are faculty problems? I began by collecting estimates of how common problems actually were for midcareer, disillusioned faculty. I wanted to learn about frequencies, variations, and benignity of symptoms. After a year of inquiries across two study campuses, I decided that departmental chairpeople were best suited to make these diagnoses. They, more than anyone else, were in a position to know which colleagues evidenced dysphoria, social and professional isolation, and oppositionalism to departmental functioning, and generated the most complaints from students. In particular, they seemed best attuned to who was or was not meeting usual career expectations held by departments in terms of collegial respect, student respect, and self-respect.

In one inquiry, I met with fifty chairpeople from a research and a comprehensive campus to have them discuss and rate their departmental colleagues (total $N = 919$). My prior surveys of chairs suggested the following list of problems exhibited by disillusioned colleagues (rank-ordered in terms of chairs' offhand predictions of commonality). These faculty members were:

1. Socially isolated from their colleagues
2. Regularly unfriendly toward their chairperson
3. Uncooperative or oppositional in departmental meetings and at other functions (for example, by disparaging the department to job candidates)
4. Inactive as researchers/scholars
5. Frequent sources of student complaints
6. Unwilling to share work on committees or to do student advising
7. Explosive with students and colleagues
8. Suspicious, obsessive, even paranoid.

As they reflected on the characteristics of the individual faculty members who fell under one or more of these categories, chairs confirmed this catalogue of problem types. For the most common of categories, such as isolationism and oppositionalism, estimates averaged around one-third of the roughly six hundred more-senior faculty (those twelve years or more post–Ph.D.). Estimates for relatively junior faculty, in contrast, averaged less than one-third of that for midcareer colleagues. Patterns were similar across campuses.

Even the least common characteristics, of explosiveness and suspiciousness, still produced substantial estimates of occurrence. Chairs saw around

one-fifth of their more-senior faculty as problematically explosive or suspicious. Chairs designated fewer but still notable numbers of junior faculty in the same categories, again at about one-third the rate of seniors.

When I convened four groups of chairs (two on each campus; all with about fifteen members) to reflect on these results, several trends of conversation emerged in each of the meetings. The first response was always a humorous sense of relief that these problems were common across most departments; most chairpeople had believed their own departments to be nearly unique in experiencing moderate-to-high levels of problem faculty. The second pair of realizations followed from the first: For one thing, chairs had rarely talked to other chairs about their problem faculty members (even though faculty misbehaviors in general and the suspiciousness/explosiveness of a few faculty members in particular contributed the most to thoughts of quitting as chair of the department). For another thing, chairs could find useful support and information in sharing experiences about faculty problems.

Other insights from chairpeople also emerged in predictable fashion. One was surprise at the commonality of problems. About one-third of veteran faculty members had been deemed unsociable and oppositional; nearly two-thirds did not shoulder their fair share of such department responsibilities as student advising. The reason, chairs surmised, was the natural temptation to attend to more positive matters in day-to-day operations of chairing. Another surprise lay in the incidence of problems for junior faculty; while newcomers did not qualify as problematic at the levels just cited, many of them appeared to be well on their way to patterns of disillusionment. For example, over 15 percent had become significantly isolated from campus colleagues and almost 40 percent were shirking departmental duties, including student advising. The "sleeper" in these compilations for the chairs first seeing them concerned scholarly inactivity. Almost no one had, prior to specifying individual colleagues with problems, imagined that unproductivity would be the most common problem (70 percent of seniors, 48 percent of juniors). More important, in the view of the chairs, no one had realized the pervasiveness of scholarly silence and procrastination among junior faculty. Chairs also had an explanation for this oversight: their own shortcomings in productivity made them overlook the topic wherever convenient.

One discussion point always brought out the most involvement and excitement. All the chairs agreed that the most troublesome aspects of problematic midcareer colleagues were their explosiveness and suspiciousness. These attributes were most wearing on chairpeople. They were also most costly for colleagues and departments. Explosive and suspicious faculty, chairs agreed, took up the most time for memos, meetings, and phone calls, often in the evenings and on weekends. These colleagues did the most to undermine collegiality and morale. And these same explosive and suspicious faculty seemed to exact the greatest toll on students who reported having been mistaught and harassed in their classes.

There were more accounts of misbehaviors in these cathartic discussions, but the enduring point was this: once the aforementioned groups of chairs had met and confirmed the enormity of faculty problems that occur in from 10 to 30 percent of faculty members, they were primed to help me convince higher administrators that faculty development programs for midcareer, disillusioned colleagues were needed and overdue. In fact, chairpeople typically made a far better case than I could have. They were able to present the costs of disillusioned midcareer colleagues in personal and departmental terms. They spiced their accounts with reminders of the prices that departments were paying with oppositional colleagues, many of whom would likely hang on at the periphery for twenty years or more before retiring. And chairs began to describe themselves in the role of faculty developers who could help translate my plans into reality.

Question 2: To what do problem faculty attribute their midcareer disillusionment? With the data from question 1, I met again with the same fifty individual chairs to enlist their help in deciding on the criteria for faculty to be labeled as middle-aged and disillusioned (MADFs). These were the problem individuals most in need of a renewal program. We settled on a reliably ratable configuration of these qualities: (1) disengagement from department and profession; (2) unproductivity as scholars, researchers, and creators; (3) disillusionment with career progress and self-worth; and (4) isolation from colleagues and students.

Chairs were able to identify 164 midcareer faculty as qualifying on all four dimensions. From those, I selected a representative sample for interviewing, one that I could match with a sample of midcareer faculty designated as exemplary performers. By avoiding public labels for either group, I was able to moderate the discomfort that might have gone with membership in this first group; while interviewing both groups, I simply informed individuals that I was interested in constructing a general picture of what shaped professorial careers. All sixty-six faculty (thirty-three of them MADFs) participated in thoroughly disclosive fashion, sometimes after displays of initial skepticism.

Two striking qualities emerged from my hour-long interviews in the offices of these midcareer faculty. First, the most embittered of complaints (almost all of them from MADFs) concerned surprises. Faculty members felt their careers had been derailed through their (1) not having been informed of what was expected and rewarded during formative years on campus; (2) feeling rejected and unappreciated by colleagues, notably in seemingly grudging decisions for renewal and tenure; (3) disapproval by students and lack of rewards for teaching; (4) unfair, discouraging treatment by granting agencies and by editors of scholarly publications; and (5) perhaps most telling, public embarrassment on campus (for example, being called up before a campus disciplinary committee).

The exemplary group, in contrast, said little about surprises and a lot about opportunities for growth. What struck me in collecting and analyzing these accounts of career turning points was not just that career paths were so strikingly different for the two groups. I was fascinated with the possibility that the most crucial of events had happened within the first few years of their professorial lives. If the turning points were as rapid and simple as they appeared to be, perhaps faculty developers could realistically help prevent some of them.

Question 3: Do the most crucial turning points occur quickly in professorial careers? While admirable precedents exist for studying the career development process for professors (Baldwin and Blackburn, 1981; Blackburn and Havighurst, 1979), none had focused systematically on early events. More important, none had looked for the locations of what Clark (1987) called "career fault lines."

My own attempts to establish reliable accounts of primary turning points meandered through a series of other experiments. In every case my original sense of primacy effects was confirmed; as midcareer faculty reflected on turning points in their careers, they invariably attributed more and more significance to events that happened during their initial years on campus. To reconstruct these primal events, I settled on a modification of a technique from cognitive psychology called retrospective thinking aloud protocols (Perkins, 1981). As I use it, this strategy immerses subjects in repeated exercises of reporting (contrasted to explaining) the thoughts and feelings that accompanied crucial events. In the course of several meetings where individual faculty reconstructed the most telling of career turning points, a report of a crucial event often went like this:

> I had only been on campus for two months when I attended a meeting of the faculty senate on my own. I approached someone from my own department at the back of the room, someone I barely knew. As I began to reintroduce myself to him, he suddenly turned and walked away. I felt totally rejected. I thought to myself: I'll never be accepted here . . . no point in trying. I left the meeting and went for a walk and thought over the other slights and put-offs I had experienced since coming to campus. Never again did I make the effort to be a part of things.

By the end of a year of repeating at least three reconstructions from scratch, participants spontaneously reduced their lists of turning points to three, four, or five events. Each such event consisted of a specific, memorable experience of thoughts and feelings, not to generally positive or negative trends. The commonality of the resulting lists permitted me to draw up model career patterns for both disillusioned and exemplary faculty at midcareer, presented in Table 3.1 (turning points are listed in their usual order of occurrence).

Table 3.1. Model Career Experiences for Disillusioned and Exemplary Faculty

MADFs	Exemplars
1. collegial isolation/neglect	1. ready social networks
2. collegial disapproval	2. finding success in grants/publications
3. self-doubts about competence	3. gaining acceptance with students
4. feeling victimized, suspicious	4. opportunities for consulting/travel

Evidently, the hypothesis was confirmed: turning points for adaptive or maladaptive patterns that persisted into midcareers did seem to have occurred within the first few years on campus. Few of the crucial events in final lists represented incidents beyond tenure decisions; most came within the first two years after initial contact with the campus.

I have found other confirmations of these results. This same general set of turning points has held for other samples of midcareer faculty whom I have studied. And almost identical patterns of fault lines or success experiences appear for samples of new faculty still in their first few years on campus (Boice, 1992). Clearly, it seems to me, career directions are cast with startling rapidity.

But what value lies in this identification of turning points? One clue emerges from the study of faculty still in their initial years. There, the most vulnerable individuals are nontraditional faculty. Women and minorities among new faculty are most likely to come to campus without social networks and mentoring already in place. They, more than white males, suffer feelings of isolation and disapproval; they, more than traditional newcomers, evidence symptoms of stress and are most likely to leave campus for nonacademic careers. Thus, one thing that these turning points can tell us concerns differential vulnerability: the new faculty we work hardest to recruit and need most to retain are most in peril of these career fault lines.

Another thing this sort of analysis suggests is that usual turning points of the negative sort may be economically avoidable. We may owe it to ourselves and our new hires to work harder at prearranging social networks and initial successes at teaching than we typically do.

But what about renewal and redirection later on, with midcareer faculty seemingly set in their ways? What value lies in uncovering their fault lines? Are cynics realistic in their dismissal of "deadwood" from faculty development plans? In the remaining part of this chapter I will describe preliminary attempts to use this information about early turning points in programs of renewal.

Two Faculty Development Strategies for MADFs

I began with the assumption that the same programs proven effective for new faculty might work for midcareer, disillusioned colleagues. To assume other-

wise would be to accept the notion that initial socialization and habits were irreversible; I tried to leave my most deterministic beliefs behind when I abandoned my career in ethology.

Mentoring. So, for example, given that it had proved helpful to arrange mentoring and collaboration for new hires (Boice, 1992), why not expect similar interventions to work for midcareer faculty? The intervention was simple but seemingly risky. I recruited a mix of ten midcareer faculty, half of them MADFs and half exemplary, as mentors for new faculty. Because neither group of seniors had clear ideas of how to mentor, we relied on group meetings of mentoring pairs to build a sense of appropriate activities (for example, occasional modeling and collaboration in teaching, and clarification of what the most successful new faculty routinely do as teachers, colleagues, and scholarly writers).

To the surprise of onlookers (and of MADFs themselves), almost all the mentors proved helpful in arranging supports and resources for new faculty. Their mentoring helped protégés achieve clear advantages, including higher student ratings for teaching and higher rates of writing productivity compared to unmentored new faculty. Moreover, both groups of mentors judged themselves to be the primary beneficiaries of the experience. While MADFs commented more on things that might have helped them make happier and more adaptive beginnings as junior faculty, they joined other mentors in seeing the readiness with which they could adapt the advice they had collected for protégés for themselves. This was, first and foremost, an occasion for rethinking and redirecting one's already mature career, no matter how ostensibly successful.

Because, for instance, MADFs had collaborators in teaching (with their protégés) and in the experience of enjoyable discussions about teaching improvement (in monthly meetings of mentoring pairs), they became more collegial. Many of them expressed the phenomenon in words such as this: "This is the first time that I have felt a real part of campus." And, to cite one more example, because their role in championing protégés pushed mentors into meetings with chairpeople and departmental committees, formerly isolated MADFs found face-saving and comfortable means for reengagement in the vital business of their departments and campuses.

Cataloguing. In an older, still ongoing series of programs (Boice, 1986), I enlisted chairpeople and MADFs as partners in a kind of growth contracting for renewal. One study involved fifty-three midcareer faculty designated by their chairs as MADFs; forty-four of them volunteered for at least a year of participation (with prospects of meaningful incentives such as merit pay raises and/or promotion to professor). Of those forty-four, only nine failed to stay the course.

Their contracts with chairpeople included structured plans for coteaching with a colleague and for maintaining a catalogue of current activities and future plans for collegiality, teaching, and scholarship (Boice, 1992). One

purpose of "cataloguing" (midcareer faculty tend to dislike the term "growth contracting") was to encourage clear and realistic plans for renewal plus definable milestones for progress with identified supports and resources. "Balance" and "moderation" were the bywords.

Another purpose was to lend structure and direction to the biweekly meetings that chairs and their partners held. With time, at most a couple of months, involvement and bonding were reported by both pair members. Faculty who had been described as intractable were seen in a kindlier, more optimistic light; chairs who had seemed disapproving and unfair became allies and even friends.

The results of this cataloguing project speak for themselves: Of the thirty-five stayers, thirty-two charted significant progress toward all four primary goals: (1) reestablishing comfortable and cordial relationships with a majority of departmental colleagues; (2) reengaging in scholarship about their disciplinary specialty and about teaching improvement; (3) supplanting their old styles of thinking pessimistically; and (4) reinvolving themselves in departmental responsibility (starting with active and nondisruptive participation in departmental meetings).

Can We Avoid Disillusionment in the Academy?

When each of these projects was well underway, the participants themselves posed an important question. They asked, Why do we so rarely figure out what derails the careers of so many faculty, all of whom began with strong promise? Or they asked, Why do we so uncommonly offer help to the faculty most in need of it?

Curiously, the participants, both the chairpeople and the midcareer faculty, provided the readiest and best answers. Bright individuals that they are, professors quickly saw the values of reflecting on previously unexamined careers. They supposed, first of all, that the sink-or-swim atmosphere of academe militates against scrutinizing reasons for failure. Folklore leads us to believe that academicians with the right stuff will survive. Early on, we learn not to inquire or complain for fear of appearing weak in a setting that values autonomy and individualism above all.

But then the conversations took on a dramatic swing. First the mood turned somber. Midcareer faculty, whether still disillusioned or growing more optimistic, saw themselves as part of the problem: early in their careers, they admitted, they could have done more to be active in soliciting collegiality and in acquiring knowledge about professorial success usually kept tacit. And more recently, they added, they could have been more receptive to ideas of renewal; no one, they discovered, had been more skeptical about prospects of reviving "deadwood" than they.

With more discussion, the mood turned happier and more hopeful. Midcareer faculty and their chairpeople recognized that renewal is better late

than never. A consensus emerged: no matter about prior misconceptions and missed opportunities, the solution lay in persisting in a forward-looking program of renewal. Moments such as these, even with the inevitable interludes of disappointment, are the stuff that keep me enthusiastic about practicing faculty development. How they affect my own aging face and career is still a matter of daily inquiry.

References

Baldwin, R. G., and Blackburn, R. T. "The Academic Career as a Development Process." *Journal of Higher Education*, 1981, 52, 598–614.

Blackburn, R. T., and Havighurst, R. J. "Career Patterns of Male Social Scientists." *Higher Education*, 1979, 8, 553–572.

Boice, R. "Faculty Development Via Field Programs for Middle-Aged, Disillusioned Faculty." *Research in Higher Education*, 1986, 25, 115–135.

Boice, R. *The New Faculty Member.* San Francisco: Jossey-Bass, 1992.

Boice, R. "New Faculty Involvement of Women and Minorities." *Research in Higher Education*, in press.

Clark, B. R. *The Academic Life: Small Worlds, Different Worlds.* Princeton, N.J.: Carnegie Foundation for the Advancement of Teaching, 1987.

Perkins, D. N. *The Mind's Best Work.* Cambridge, Mass.: Harvard University Press, 1981.

ROBERT BOICE *is professor of psychology at the State University of New York, Stony Brook.*

Over the past decade King's College has redesigned the faculty reward system, mixing intrinsic and extrinsic incentives in three interrelated initiatives: general education reform, senior faculty performance appraisal, and merit pay. This chapter chronicles the process of meaningfully changing faculty roles and rewards.

Designing a Reward System to Promote the Career Development of Senior Faculty

Donald W. Farmer

In the past decade King's College has redesigned its faculty reward system to accomplish two critical objectives. First, curricular reform—a time-honored vehicle for tapping *intrinsic* faculty commitments to development in their discipline—has been wedded to significant changes in personnel policies—the time-honored source of *extrinsic* incentives for faculty performance. Second, performance appraisal and compensation policies have been built upon intrinsic faculty commitments to uniquely reinforce organizational support for faculty development as teachers. I will begin with a brief background sketch, and then I will focus on the mix of intrinsic and extrinsic incentives that have been combined in three distinct but interrelated initiatives: outcomes-based general education, senior faculty performance appraisal, and merit pay. I will conclude with an overview of faculty response to date and a distillation of the lessons we have learned.

Background

During the 1970s and early 1980s, King's College, an undergraduate, Carnegie classification Comprehensive College II, located in northeastern Pennsylvania and enrolling 1,800 full-time students and 550 part-time students, found itself in an increasingly vulnerable position: a heavily tenured but relatively young full-time faculty of one hundred—hired for the most part in the late 1960s—was confronting a new student body with substantial skill deficits. Originally hired as a teaching faculty, they found themselves

uneasily responding to the curricular and pedagogical challenges of the new academic age. Three ad hoc study groups from the faculty had reviewed the general education program during the 1970s and identified glaring weaknesses, but action to rectify these weaknesses had not been taken. Individual academic departments were neither adopting new instructional methods nor reflecting in their course offerings the latest developments within their disciplines.

In this context, at the request of the college's board of directors, the president established the position of director of planning as part of the senior administration in 1974. After twelve years of serving as a faculty member, I was appointed to this position and accepted the board's mandate to become the college's change agent. The mandate of the new planning office was simple: *bring King's College to the "cutting edge" of change in American higher education.* A number of initiatives were undertaken in the ensuing decade (1974–84), including creating a comprehensive faculty development program; bringing national workshops on teaching and learning issues to campus; designing a contractual faculty professional development day; and actively seeking out participation as a pilot campus in national projects (for example, the American Association for Higher Education [AAHE] National Assessment Forum). When the chief academic officer left the college in 1984, the ensuing search served as a kind of referendum on the college's future. Both the then-new president, drawn from the development side of the ledger, and the faculty search committee self-consciously opted for the internal "change" candidate: the director of planning.

With the groundwork already laid, the next eight years saw three major initiatives emanating from the Academic Affairs office: general education reform, course-embedded assessment, and reform of faculty evaluation and compensation policies. Taken together, in less than a decade these three initiatives have changed the "tone" of the faculty (to use the characterization of a chemistry professor who currently chairs the faculty council): "They [the faculty] are more likely to try new things . . . and there's a sense of intellectual revitalization." While varying widely in their immediate impetus and in faculty response, what connects these initiatives most concretely is administrative leadership in building incentives and opportunities for senior faculty members to fulfill essential career development needs in a static employment market.

Renewing the curriculum has long been recognized as a tested, effective vehicle through which to harness faculty energies in the service of institutional goals. Beyond the prototypical turf battles among departments, the curriculum taps the most basic disciplinary and professional commitments that bring professors into an academic career. Less widely recognized have been the possibilities for structuring basic personnel policies—faculty evaluation, promotion, and compensation practices—that build upon those same basic faculty commitments in the service of promoting and enhancing insti-

tutional vitality. The story that follows is in one sense that of energetic administrative leadership. More fundamentally, however, it is the story of the senior faculty themselves, and of the incentives that are basic to their career development and the real possibilities for enlightened institutional policy to build upon those incentives to the benefit of everyone.

Curriculum Reform and Intrinsic Faculty Commitments

Three abortive attempts to reform general education requirements over the previous decade suggested the need for an intensive, hands-on approach to intervention. Over a two-year period, I met monthly with the curriculum and teaching committee, who took upon themselves the responsibility for forming faculty project teams in a variety of subject areas in general education. These teams were charged with developing entirely new courses that were geared to the achievement of specific student learning outcomes. Summer stipends were made available to that end for project team leaders.

No existing courses from the old curriculum continued to be offered, since the design of the new courses required that faculty first identify the desired learning outcomes for students—that is, what students should know and be able to do—with respect to each area of learning included in the new general education curriculum. Only after arriving at such a consensus did faculty project teams design each course syllabus, and, most significantly, address pedagogical strategies most likely to facilitate student achievement of the desired outcomes. Five years' worth of faculty development programs and national workshops on teaching and learning brought to the college's campus had prepared the faculty to understand the relationship of pedagogy to desired student learning outcomes. Several areas in the curriculum were designed to be interdisciplinary, and were developed by faculty project teams that crossed departmental lines (Farmer, 1988).

This two-year process of reviewing general education changed the conversation at King's College. For the faculty, it brought to center stage fundamental questions relating to their philosophy of education, course content, assessment of student learning, and the relationship between teaching strategies and student learning. Senior faculty played a leading role not only in curriculum design, but in training their colleagues to promote more active forms of student learning. These activities included programs in writing, speaking, critical thinking, and computer literacy across the curriculum. Faculty also became involved in rethinking assignments, examinations, and the use of class time.

Performance-Based Assessment. An important part of general education renewal at King's College was the design of performance-based assessment strategies. Faculty needed to begin to think about the assessment of student learning in the context of designing an activity that permitted students to apply prior learning to a new stimulus.

One of the most challenging aspects of the assessment activity has been developing and communicating assessment criteria so that students can understand and use them to improve their own progress as learners. Sharing assessment criteria with students in advance of the actual learning experience has enabled both teachers and students to develop shared expectations of student performance and has provided a framework for giving students specific and meaningful feedback about their learning.

Classroom Research. Three years into its general education program revision, the college was offered the opportunity of participating in the then-new national classroom research and assessment project led by K. Patricia Cross and Thomas Angelo. That external opportunity bolstered the internal curriculum initiative. The two actually functioned as micro- and macro-dimensions of the same task: to discover more about the relationship of faculty teaching activities to student learning in order to make changes in those teaching activities. Both support assessment as integral parts of the teaching-learning process; both support the pursuit of systematic inquiry into what, how, and how well students are learning. The particular advantage of classroom research is that it focuses explicitly on a single faculty member's classroom, an important factor since faculty are inclined to act most decisively on information about their own students and their own class (Farmer, 1991, p. 28). It also helped faculty to understand the concept of assessment as learning since they discovered concretely that good performance-based assessment strategies are also good teaching strategies.

Faculty Response. Over the two-year period nearly 40 percent of the faculty participated on project teams. Responding to a survey, faculty reported that though the process was enormously labor-intensive, they were persuaded that their students were now meeting higher academic expectations. The words of two faculty members are representative of their colleagues:

> Making course goals and assessment criteria explicit at the beginning of the course contributes to communicating clearer expectations for student learning.

> Explaining to students what is expected in a course and the strategies to help them meet these expectations communicates a concern for their success.

The process of renewing the curriculum provides intrinsic rewards by motivating and revitalizing a teaching faculty who take pride in improving student learning. As Clark (1987, p. 222) notes, faculty belief that education offers the best hope for improving the human condition creates a *sustaining myth* in which faculty believe they possess "a supreme position of great power that echoes with a sense of calling."

Senior Faculty Performance Appraisal

Unlike general education, the impetus for senior faculty review came directly from the board of directors. A majority of faculty at King's considered themselves "locked in rank" because they had reached the top salary step and were faced with the prospect of being limited to annual cost-of-living increases. The board felt, in response, that if the faculty were going to be compensated beyond the prescribed steps in rank, that some form of performance assessment based on recognized criteria was required. At the board's direction, the president developed a faculty compensation proposal that combined performance assessment and merit pay. The faculty then expressed its overwhelming opposition to this concept.

Armed with firsthand knowledge of growth contracting at Gordon College in the late 1970s, and my own experience with pilot efforts at King's College in the early 1980s, I sought to reshape the proposal to win faculty approval by separating the issue of senior faculty review from the issue of merit pay. The former was to be primarily *formative/developmental* in nature and *mandatory;* the latter was to involve *summative* assessment but be entirely *voluntary.* Moreover, the faculty was to have a decisive role in shaping the design and operational details of both programs. I met frequently with the faculty council's professional affairs committee that ultimately drafted the proposal. The decision was made to self-consciously avoid the term *post-tenure review.* The idea of a formative evaluation appealed to the faculty in part because of the favorable evaluation of a faculty growth plan pilot tested earlier. The faculty council quite correctly insisted, "We don't want to get rid of people; we want to bring them back."

The proposal that emerged was for a five-year cycle of mandatory senior faculty review, involving at King's College approximately twelve to fifteen faculty each year. Only those faculty contemplating retirement over the coming two years were eligible for exemption—an indirect, although not entirely unintended, incentive to retirement for some. At its core was a review team including the faculty member's chair, dean, two or three colleagues, and myself. Each member of the team visits the faculty member's classes, and then reviews his or her self-reflective statement, professional dossier, and ideas developed for a five-year professional growth plan. The team comes together for an hour to meet with the faculty member and provide feedback. I prepare a summary of that meeting, which then serves as the basis for subsequent conversations between the faculty member and his or her dean.

This conversation encourages faculty to continue to experiment in the classroom with new teaching strategies, to reflect more deeply on the relationship between teaching and learning, and to enlarge the definition of public scholarship appropriate for a teaching faculty. Most important, the conversation moves beyond appraisal of past performance to the

development of a professional growth plan. Such a plan frequently incorporates specific goals that serve as a basis for a subsequent sabbatical leave proposal. Each faculty member's professional growth plan, when approved by the academic vice president, is supported by a grant of $3,500 beyond regular faculty development funding levels to underwrite the specific activities set forth in the plan. Although these funds provide an extrinsic reward for senior faculty, it is clear that even more powerful intrinsic rewards are at work; indeed, many faculty devise professional growth plans that do not require utilizing the designated funds.

Faculty Response. The faculty's response to senior faculty review began with pervasive opposition, expressed freely and even eloquently at meetings of the full faculty. The tide appears to be turning, however, as the result of experience with the new system. An anonymous survey of the more than two dozen faculty who have actually undergone review over the program's first two years shows that most respond positively, especially to the professional growth plan component. Seven illustrative comments drive home this point:

Receiving praise from faculty colleagues about the quality of my teaching is energizing.

Reviewing the work of a faculty colleague who has mastered the art of teaching motivated me to be more inventive in my own classes.

No one had ever before seriously discussed with me or even shown a particular interest in helping me to implement my own personal ideas for professional development.

Developing a professional growth plan helped to prioritize my interests and to relate them to broader institutional goals.

The positive response of academic administrators to my ideas for professional growth communicated a high degree of respect and confidence in my ability.

The willingness of administrators to expend the college's limited resources to support faculty growth plans makes the experience much more than an exercise in paper pushing.

I was embarrassed to hear colleagues praise my teaching, but I was deeply moved to know that their enthusiasm was genuine.

Our experience with senior faculty review at King's College provides additional evidence of the power of intrinsic rewards in motivating and revitalizing faculty. Senior faculty need to know that others value their commitment

to pursuing the life of the mind and to effectively challenging students to develop as independent learners. Many necessary conversations for faculty do not seem to take place either naturally or frequently in higher education. Senior faculty review stimulated just such conversations. In particular, professional growth planning responded to a strong need for autonomy that attracted most faculty to academic life in the first place. It is a strategy to release creativity by empowering faculty to personally control their own career development.

Rewarding Productivity Through Merit Pay

Whereas the senior faculty review program is required of all nonretiring tenured faculty at King's College, the performance-based compensation program (that is, merit pay) is voluntary. Nonetheless, faculty response to this program has been even more negative. Many faculty argue that merit pay forces faculty to compete against their colleagues and choose not to subject themselves to that stress. Others suspect that a merit pay plan will assign greater rewards to public scholarship than to effective teaching because such scholarship is more readily measured.

The final plan that emerged from the faculty council reflected a strong commitment to effective teaching. The level of merit increase was to be determined by the three areas in which an applicant's performance had been judged commendable by his or her dean and chair: teaching, service, and public scholarship. One-half of the maximum award was assigned to the category of effective teaching, and one-fourth was assigned to service and public scholarship, respectively. Even more telling is the provision that faculty cannot receive a merit award for either service or public scholarship unless that individual receives a merit award for effective teaching.

Thus far, twenty-seven of the eligible forty-two faculty members have applied for merit awards—an encouraging number. A just completed faculty council survey of the faculty's perception of senior faculty review and merit pay reveals strong support for the former and decisive opposition to the latter. This is, in effect, a faculty judgment of the power of intrinsic rewards as the professed motivator.

First Results from the Threefold Reform

What has been the impact to date of these three related initiatives? While faculty opposition continues regarding merit pay, nonetheless there is, as the chair of the faculty council noted above, a perceptible change in the *tone* of the faculty, a greater willingness to try new things, a greater energy, as well as some identifiable changes in behavior: some faculty have experimented with development of a teaching portfolio to better document and to reflect upon new teaching initiatives, syllabus revisions, and changes in student

assignments; some faculty have formed collegial dyads for collaboratively investigating each other's teaching (similar to the Katz model described in the Smith and Smith chapter of this volume); senior faculty have increased the number of manuscripts submitted for journal publication, especially relative to pedagogy and performance-based assessment in their disciplines; and some faculty have become more active in regional and national associations, including service on committees and in leadership roles.

While there seems to be concrete, if imprecisely documented, movement, it is clear that not all faculty are "on board." The chair of the faculty council recently estimated that about 40 percent of the faculty were responding positively, about 40 percent remained indifferent, and about 20 percent remained philosophically opposed to these initiatives when they are discussed in public forums. Viewed positively, this suggests that a substantial core group of King's College faculty is emerging in less than a decade as a self-defined corps of change agents. As an administrator, I have supported the coalescence of the corps of change agents: some were invited to serve as trainers for colleagues in faculty development activities; others were invited to design and participate in pilot tests of new teaching methods and curricula; groups of senior faculty were encouraged to attend national workshops and conferences relating to the area of their professional development activity; still others have begun to serve themselves as conference presenters and to author journal articles on their classroom experiments.

Perhaps most critically, this corps has solidified around an emergent role as mentors of the increasing ranks of new King's College faculty. After nearly two decades of virtually no new blood, the college has hired twenty-eight new faculty over the past two academic years—a function primarily of recent retirements. The corps of senior faculty sees itself increasingly as the "keepers" of the traditional but revitalized institutional teaching culture, with a responsibility for socializing new faculty into experimenting with active modes of teaching appropriate to achieving the desired student learning outcomes.

Two faculty vignettes help to illustrate the extent to which faculty at King's College have been motivated by intrinsic rewards more than by extrinsic rewards. Although they acknowledge that extrinsic rewards reflected in additional compensation are appreciated, they argue forcefully that extrinsic rewards are not the driving force behind the faculty's support of change and its commitment to improving student learning. A professor of biology made the following remarks:

> The ideas of cumulative and transferable learning in general education as well as performance-based assessment helped me to focus on what outcomes I wanted for students and how to facilitate that learning. Most importantly, I was able to overcome my preoccupation with covering material which I realized eventually was at the expense of student learning. These new perspectives provide a refreshing new look at student learning and

have revitalized my teaching. The success I had in general education courses led me to apply the same ideas to courses in the biology major program. These experiences have given me a great deal of satisfaction. I know that my teaching is effective because assessment activities demonstrate that students are meeting my expectations—The senior faculty review process was actively a celebration of my teaching effectiveness. It was affirming and reinforced the motivation provided by my involvement in curriculum and pedagogical changes.

An associate professor of English added this perspective:

> By participating in developing a curriculum focusing on student learning outcomes, I was forced to re-examine my teaching strategies. I realized that I had been primarily concerned with transferring information and covering material. Focusing on outcomes and performance-based assessment helped me to radically change my teaching strategies and to emphasize thinking and understanding. I accomplished this by involving students more actively in their own learning. I was especially motivated to change my approach to teaching by my involvement in the classroom research project. Classroom research taught me what assessment as learning really meant both for me, and my students. . . . The senior review process encouraged me to think about and to plan my future. My professional growth plan permitted me to pursue areas of development that I didn't think the college would support. The support provided by the college for attending conferences convinced me that what I was doing in my classes was more innovative and effective than the case studies presented. This motivated me to become a presenter at future conferences and to publish a journal article on my classroom strategies.

Lessons Learned in the King's College Experience

The process of senior faculty revitalization at King's College is well underway, indeed self-sustaining now. What are the lessons to be learned from our experience?

Horizons of Possibility. First is the matter of the horizon of possibility. As they move through their careers, senior faculty have both a capacity for growth and a desire for growth. Young faculty members do not embark on their careers seeking to become deadwood, nor do older faculty want to become fossils (McKeachie, 1984, p. 74). Academic administrators should not underestimate the power of intrinsic rewards for motivating senior faculty. Most faculty have chosen to pursue a vocation, not simply take a job. Although institutional size and culture have played an important role in the success of intrinsic rewards in energizing faculty at King's College, they can serve in other institutional settings as well.

Institutional Culture. Much resistance to innovation arises as a result of a perceived threat to the organization's culture rather than in reaction to the substance of the proposed change (Farmer, 1990, p. 8). It is necessary, therefore, to devise a strategy for change that does not appear to threaten the assumptions, values, feelings, and ways of working that an organization's members share. It is vitally important for a change agent to know the culture of his or her institution since change strategies that work in one organization may not work in another one. An intrinsic reward system needs to be congruent with the institutional culture. A teaching faculty is energized by actually having improved student learning.

Humanistic Management Philosophy. Academic managers need to understand senior faculty as individuals who are at different stages of their lives. They have changing needs and aspirations, frequently made more complex by midlife and midcareer crises. Some have stopped learning and growing, some just perform in predictable and routine ways, while others maintain their vitality because the things they are doing continue to excite them (Seldin, 1989, p. 23). Faculty development strategies and rewards need to be broadly conceived to meet a variety of genuine faculty needs. What motivates one person at a particular stage of life may not work for another person at a different stage. The literature on aging reveals that individuals tend to differ more as they grow older because they tend to practice and enjoy those things they do well and not practice and thus decline in abilities relating to what they do not do well (McKeachie, 1984, p. 76).

Designing a Reward System. A well-designed senior faculty review process incorporating professional growth plans should be based on the following premises:

The power of intrinsic rewards to motivate senior faculty has been traditionally undervalued.

Curriculum renewal can best energize and reward faculty when changes in pedagogy are an integral part of the process.

Formative evaluation in a collegial and positive setting serves as a better motivator than the implied threats contained in summative evaluation.

Professional growth planning responds to the strong need of faculty for autonomy, freedom, and empowerment.

Appropriate opportunities need to be provided for faculty to establish ownership of new ideas and strategies.

Senior faculty experience a high level of satisfaction by playing a leadership role in institutional change.

Senior faculty have a meaningful role, both personally and organizationally, to play in mentoring younger colleagues.

Keeping colleges and universities alive and competitive in the 1990s requires finding ways to motivate senior faculty to serve as positive role mod-

els for the younger faculty who will define higher education in the twenty-first century. Senior faculty will be increasingly challenged to strike a delicate balance between continuity in their role as guardians of institutional culture and the need to change in order to incorporate the new information communication technologies transforming education for the twenty-first century.

References

Clark, B. R. *The Academic Life*. Princeton, N.J.: Carnegie Foundation for the Advancement of Teaching, 1987.

Farmer, D. W. *Enhancing Student Learning: Emphasizing Essential Competencies in Academic Programs*. Wilkes-Barre, Pa.: King's College Press, 1988.

Farmer, D. W. "Strategies for Change." In D. W. Steeples (ed.), *Managing Change in Higher Education*. New Directions for Higher Education, no. 71. San Francisco: Jossey-Bass, 1990.

Farmer, D. W. "A Macro and Micro Approach to Classroom Research." *Educational Forum*, 1991, 2, 28–36.

McKeachie, W. J. "The Faculty as a Renewable Resource." In M. Waggoner, R. L. Alfred, and M. W. Peterson (eds.), *Academic Renewal*. Ann Arbor: University of Michigan Press, 1984.

Seldin, P. "Staying Alive." In *Conference Proceedings of the Second Conference on Professional and Personal Renewal for Faculty*. Athens: University of Georgia Press, 1989.

DONALD W. FARMER is vice president for academic affairs at King's College, Wilkes-Barre, Pennsylvania.

Fiscal threats mobilized a coalition of administrators and senior faculty on a private urban commuter campus to take action on student retention issues. Drawing on collaborative curricular models provided by the honors program, the coalition created a series of mutually reinforcing faculty development initiatives. Five years later, retention is increasing nearly as fast as faculty morale.

Building Coalitions for Faculty Revitalization: The Case of Long Island University's Brooklyn Campus

Bernice Braid

Long Island University (LIU) is a multicampus private institution primarily serving first-generation collegians. The Brooklyn campus, its oldest and only urban site, draws undergraduates largely from its metropolitan area, a magnet for recent immigrants. By the mid-1980s a combination of high attrition, associated fiscal distress, and the uncertain intentions of a new central administration threatened the continued viability of the Brooklyn campus. In response to that threat, beginning in 1986, a campus-based coalition of faculty and administrators designed a retention plan, secured the temporary support of the board of trustees for a two-year curricular pilot project, and put together a series of four major overlapping grants to support faculty development efforts that have significantly improved retention, enhanced faculty morale, and boosted the overall academic climate of the Brooklyn campus.

How was a campus divided by three faculty strikes in the previous decade "recalled to life"? And how were the energies of disaffected senior faculty harnessed as both agents and beneficiaries of the changes?

The story of LIU's Brooklyn campus is above all else a chronicle of *strategy*: the coalescence of an initially small faculty-administrative coalition in response to external threats, and the expansion of the faculty side of that coalition through specific strategic interventions aimed at redeploying already existing campus curricular structures to build overlapping communities of faculty dedicated to promoting the learning of their students.

I will begin by offering a brief overview of the institutional setting. I will then chronicle the initial impetus for faculty-administrative coalition

New Directions for Teaching and Learning, no. 55, Fall 1993 © Jossey-Bass Publishers

building, the search for models for strategic intervention, and the successful triangulation of multiple grant projects to build overlapping communities of re-energized faculty. I will conclude with a report on some early indicators of success and some reflections on lessons learned in the process.

Setting

In the context of LIU's multicampus system, students at the Brooklyn campus in particular have high levels of financial need and need-induced attrition. Virtually all work, many full-time, frequently dropping out to accumulate sufficient money to complete their education later in their lives. Familiarity with academic expectations and acquaintance with career options run predictably low. Wiser in many ways than faculty or staff, students are often inexperienced, even naive in their knowledge of what their city can offer them. Most, having had to earn their way through high school, have enjoyed little leisure in which to explore the possibilities, whether cultural or professional, of their (new) hometown.

But they have always been hungry to succeed. Early in the 1960s an outstanding higher educational opportunity program began, and by the mid-1960s a university honors program was launched; these efforts proved pivotal to the developments chronicled in this case study. Since 1965 the honors program has been a testing ground for curricular and pedagogical innovation through which several generations of faculty have filtered. With support from two generous Mellon Foundation grants, it has also sponsored occasional professional workshops for faculty. The honors program consistently included senior faculty. Both programs have operated as collaborative exceptions to a dominant campus ethos of separatism. Specifically, the honors program has utilized collaborative instruction, in the form of a required freshman course cluster, since its inception.

Faculty at LIU Brooklyn reflect the usual range of personal attributes to be expected in a metropolis. They hail from everywhere, often because of a desire to work in New York City. If tempted to leave, they often find that their academic history hinders job change, and stay. Educated traditionally themselves, senior faculty, who came to the campus eager to prepare new generations for the scholarly and professional tasks of older ones, quickly discovered their actual professional world to be a mix of the best and worst they had idealistically hoped to find.

In the mid-1980s many felt stuck, showing signs of resentment when resources ran thin, a resentment augmented by the pressure of an urban commuter campus that contrasts starkly with the suburban—even luxurious—ambiance of LIU sister residential sites. Over time these faculty began to show a tendency to be on campus only for their teaching obligations. A pattern of absenteeism evolved that expressed faculty frustration even as it exac-

erbated the tensions characteristic of organizations where access and communication have eroded.

Building a Faculty-Administrative Coalition

Faculty-administrative and interfaculty conflict had been facts of life at this unionized campus throughout the 1970s, a decade that saw three strikes. The conflicts culminated in a 1984 proposal by the president to completely reorganize LIU and to effectively vest all control in a remote central administration on Long Island.

This initial call to arms waited only for the opportunity provided by the coming of a new university president in 1986 to find a focus. Among his very first acts was to retain an outside consulting firm to thoroughly review university operations. This firm surveyed alumni, continuing students, stopouts, dropouts, and no-shows. A composite profile of attitude and financial need emerged that spurred university officers to focus single-mindedly on the issue of student retention. In announcing the resultant LIU plan, the president urged the university to adopt an educational menu emphasizing skills development, academic support, cooperative education, and linkages to the workplace in order to engage and ultimately graduate its students.

His announcement brought with it both tremendous challenge and opportunity: each campus was to have responsibility for operationalizing the LIU plan locally. On the Brooklyn campus, that challenge fell to a faculty already alarmed by the administrative reorganization of 1986. Led by a new provost, herself a representative of the urban population on campus, and sensitive to their needs, the Brooklyn campus quickly organized a series of task forces, cochaired by administrative and faculty leaders, charged with identifying options for action. Casting student attrition as the fundamental problem, the task forces agreed on projects to support faculty development and to create a single freshman year program implemented in two stages: the planning year (1988–89), followed by a pilot year (1989–90), aimed at offering a cohesive experience centered on a required freshman orientation seminar.

This proposal for the Brooklyn campus's version of the LIU plan was brought directly to the university's board of trustees through the president. The board, for their part, agreed to provide seed money for the two-year pilot on the condition that external funds would be sought for continuing support beyond the pilot years—should the project prove successful.

The sequence of events—institution-wide assessment, institutional focus on retention, campus-based task forces, board seed money, and cochairs from faculty and administration throughout the 1987–89 period—accomplished a crucial goal. Together these moves cemented a tripartite coalition that undergirds the entire faculty development initiative now in its second year.

Searching for Models for Strategic Intervention

With the board's approval in hand, administrative responsibility for implementing the Brooklyn campus's LIU plan was assigned to the director of the honors program, an administrator experienced in course clusters, field-based learning, and faculty development workshops (thanks to the earlier Mellon grants to the honors program). This meant that responsibility for the new freshman orientation seminar planning rested with the same person who had evolved the honors program curriculum and its collaborative planning process. Her first practical task was to determine how to proceed in a fashion that cemented the evolving, but still fragile, coalition.

Ideas were drawn as much as possible from local conventions. Two pivotal activities of the honors program surfaced as useable models: *faculty workshops* that explored active pedagogical strategies in interactive ways, and *curriculum design* of the honors freshman sequence, since 1965 framed as a course cluster of three yearlong classes in English, history, and philosophy. This cluster, organized around a unifying theme for the entire year, requires faculty to imagine their syllabi as tandem instruments of curricular implementation. It presumes that occasional assignments will be read by instructors from more than one discipline. It assumes further that at regular intervals all faculty and students will take part in joint seminar-workshops in which they as a group will examine topics and texts from all disciplinary viewpoints represented. Given a full year's time with a constant student population, faculty have an exceptional opportunity to witness and encourage student growth, and unusual latitude to craft structured field explorations to enrich the entire cluster.

Fundamental to both these faculty workshops and the cluster curricular design is the principle of *collaborative planning*. Decisions about themes, texts, approaches, and joint cross-disciplinary seminars are made in annual two-day sessions attended by all faculty teaching in the program, a group that always includes at least some carryover personnel from the previous year. Because of yearly planning and participant continuity, there is ample occasion for colleagues to witness evolution in each other's practices and attitudes. Hence the program provides a clear record of tangible change experienced over time, and establishes dramatically, during the planning sessions, that changes occur as a result of the *collaborative process* itself.

One final dimension of the honors program model is its objective to build a community of learners. This is accomplished by establishing a physical "home" for students and faculty, by extensive use of *structured explorations* and *field-based learning* (Braid, 1990, pp. 93–105), and by tackling hard social issues directly in its first-year courses. Hence the program has successfully moved the challenge of socially diverse students from mere "environment" to the stuff of intellectual debate, that is, to course content. Through the use of themes, it has incorporated complex and contradictory issues, such as race

and identity, into freshman coursework, making matters of perspective one of the foundations of the program. Tight course clusters stretch the boundaries of disciplinary discourse for students, and the collaborative process imposed on faculty by clusters and course-related fieldtrips has stretched the boundaries of their professional collegial interactions.

With the honors program as a visible indigenous model, the newly emergent freshman orientation seminar (OS) has found it easy to adopt aspects of the earlier structure to a broader constituency. *Planning* occurs in daylong instructors' workshops, themselves interactive, which offer a collaborative experience to each semester's "team." *Assigned partners* work together to shape their syllabi to accommodate occasional joint sessions with both groups of students. *Monthly meetings* encourage instructors to share their most inventive teaching strategies, and to seek one another's counsel on intractable or unanticipated problems.

The OS course invites students to address the same serious issues dealt with in the honors program. Under the overall rubric of "The University: Discovery and Change," faculty can be flexible in response to particular classes, even as they help students confront "change" and experience "discovery." Workshops and meetings alike are rooted in the direct experience of structured explorations. All OS sections begin the term, on orientation day, with a three-hour laboratory that sends small teams out into the world to "collect information" of specific kinds as an introduction to the process of gathering data, interpreting it, analyzing it in a social context, and presenting it in a public arena.

This approach to inquiry and systematic analysis of acquired information is the same structured exploration used in honors program fieldwork. Fieldtrips, which stress focus, intentionality, and reflection, are now part of the architecture of the honors program, OS, and increasingly of other courses on campus. Prior preparation, exploring, recording data, and analyzing records reveal to students the nature and role of context in making sense of the world, and puts them at the center of their own learning. Through written observations and self-reflective essays utilized as classroom texts, students develop a sense of how they themselves process information, and what the role of "pattern" is in understanding a complex world.

Triangulation of Convergent Grant Projects

The OS program, the most inclusive project from a faculty viewpoint, is in its third year of formal institutionalization. Fully endorsed after the pilot project year, it has produced an experienced cohort of about 40 percent of instructional staff, all of whom have participated in both collaborative planning workshops and monthly meetings. The evolution of honors course clusters has continued, and Mellon-funded faculty development workshops, co-sponsored by the honors program and either arts and sciences or the faculty

Figure 5.1. A Chronological Overview of the Faculty Development Grants of the Brooklyn Campus of Long Island University

Year	Spring	Fall
1991	*AAC Project* Course cluster planning year: Team 1 starts (Total = 2 faculty)	*AAC Project* Course cluster planning year: Teams 1 and II (Total = 4 faculty) *Title III Project* Cohort 1 starts (Total = 10 faculty, including 4 AAC faculty)
1992	*AAC Project* Course cluster planning year: Teams I, II, & III (Total = 6 faculty) *Title III Project* Cohort 1 continues *Pew Project* Cohort 1 starts (19 participants including AAC Team III)	*AAC Project* Pilot Project starts (Teams I, II, & III). Nonparticipating faculty discuss possibility of new clusters *Title III Project* Cohort 2 starts (10 new faculty added) *Pew Project* Cohort 2 starts (16 new faculty added; 13 carryovers)
1993	*AAC Project* Pilot Project ends (Teams I, II, & III) *Title III Project* Cohort 2 continues *Pew Project* Cohort 2 continues. New faculty added *NEH Project* Cohort 1 starts (Total = 18 faculty, incl. 4 Title III and 4 Pew faculty)	*AAC Project* Refinement of clusters begun in Fall '92. Beginning of clusters discussed in Fall '92 *Title III Project* Cohort 3 starts *Pew Project* Cohort 3 starts; new faculty added *NEH Project* Possible renewal of funding
1994	*AAC Project* Take course cluster to general faculty for approval and implementation *Title III Project* Cohort 3 continues *Pew Project* Last funded semester. Cohort 3 continues; some new faculty added *NEH Project* Possible renewal of funding	*Title III Project* Cohort 4 starts *Pew Project* Possible renewal of funding *NEH Project* Possible renewal of funding
1995	*Title III Project* Cohort 4 continues *Pew Project* Possible renewal of funding	*Title III Project* Cohort 5 starts *Pew Project* Possible renewal of funding
1996	*Title III Project* Cohort 5 continues *Pew Project* Possible renewal of funding	

The AAC "Engaging Cultural Legacies" Project pairs English and history in a yearlong "minicluster" course pilot that incorporates English and history core requirements. The project uses elements from the university honors program, freshman orientation seminar (OS). Periodic seminars integrate the course across disciplinary lines.

The USDE Title III Grant Project introduces new educational orientations (for example, educational technology) to faculty to assist their efforts to revise the core curricula.

The Pew Professional Development Project addresses the development of essential literacies, multicultural perspectives, and experience-based (active) learning strategies. The project revitalizes teaching on the Brooklyn campus through the transformation of pedagogical approaches, classroom strategies, and course syllabi.

The NEH Faculty Development Seminars in Non-Western Classics prepares faculty to design and teach cross-cultural courses. It uses the honors core sequence as a "lab" for material to be applied to campuswide core syllabi.

senate, have occurred periodically since 1984. The crucial shift of focus and priority resulting from the board of trustee's challenge to the Brooklyn campus paved the way for a flurry of concurrent, externally funded faculty development projects now underway.

Four parallel efforts, each deriving some or all their objectives and methods from programs described above as models, are currently in place. These convergent projects are (1) the Association of American Colleges' (AAC) Cultural Legacies Project (Spring 1991–Fall 1993); (2) U.S. Department of Education (USDE) Title III Project (1991–96); (3) Pew Faculty Development Project (1991–94); and (4) National Endowment for the Humanities (NEH) Faculty Development Project (Spring 1993–Fall 1993). (See the timeline included in Figure 5.1.) The single common denominator for all these grants is their focus on faculty development as it affects quality of instruction and curricular applications.

Chronologically, the first of these parallel efforts is the AAC Cultural Legacies Project. It has exposed its participants, during their own planning phase (1991–92), to innovations in core curriculum elsewhere; brought experts to campus as consultants; and drawn faculty and administration into direct working collaboration. Funding is provided for travel to conferences for faculty and for site visits by the principal consultant. Three teams, each composed of faculty from the English and history departments, have spent this year developing for mainstream students a pilot minicluster modeled on the honors course cluster. It introduces into the core varied and viable treatments of multiple cultures, in ways that embrace interactive learning strategies practiced in faculty workshops. It seeks to include some field experience where appropriate. The pilot minicluster project, for which preregistration response has been surprisingly strong, has begun.

As faculty development this opportunity accomplishes much. The three teams have met several times, and together have presented their ideas to the campus curriculum committee. They have met with the assigned consultant and benefited from explaining to him their objectives and methods. Moreover, the team members overlap within the two parallel efforts: one team is included in the Pew Faculty Development Project (see below), and the other two are in the U.S. Department of Education Title III Project (see below), which means that there is an automatic mechanism through which both projects connect and can hear about one another.

The second of the parallel efforts is a large five-year USDE Title III Project with two activities. One of them is a systematic expansion of academic advising and support services along lines reflecting a holistic approach to student learning. Advising is organized with an emphasis on OS as seminal to personal growth, and therefore builds on the pivotal role of that seminar as workshop training. The grant provides funding to add student mentors, increase workshop training sessions, and add needed staff. Funding allows a degree of integration of academic advising and curricular practices woven

into the fabric of new courses, themselves increasingly the product of collective planning.

The second major activity of the USDE Title III Project is faculty development. Funds support interactive teaching, enhanced classroom use of technology, such as interactive computer uses tailored to particular course content, and provide equipment for a faculty resources room. There is some inclusion of efforts to diversify course content and encourage use of non-Western texts.

Most AAC minicourse cluster team members are part of the initial cohort of the USDE Title III grant. The resource room alone is explicit acknowledgment of the collaborative thrust of these convergent projects: it will service currently funded participants, eventually supporting all faculty to collaborate on teaching projects. Essentially, it provides a space for unexpected encounters of the creative kind, effectively making the experience of collaborative learning concrete. At one level this reflects adherence to grant guidelines; at another, the resource room's central location and inclusiveness express the spirit of faculty development projects at this juncture. Emphasizing that the "problem of retention" has guided all development activity guarantees a focus on classroom utilization of new academic ideas and approaches to teaching. This emphasis also encourages partnerships between faculty and staff who provide student support services like academic advising (funded through activity I of Title III).

AAC team members not among senior faculty in the USDE Title III Project are funded by the Pew Charitable Trusts Faculty Development Project. This three-year activity, now in its second year, supports senior faculty and some adjuncts. It focuses directly on interactive learning strategies, like small-group work and discursive instruction, and applies them to the challenge of cultural diversity embedded in course content. Since members of both the AAC and USDE Title III projects cohorts attend conferences and workshops with the Pew cohort, and since some individual projects cut across the boundaries of all grants, there is a heady mix of ideas and cross-fertilization evident in each session. The annual report, complete with appendixes that illustrate just how aware faculty are of their own engagement in the development process, provides remarkable evidence that participants see themselves as learners in a collaborative framework. Documentation, including trial runs of exercises, their Pew portfolio, and self-assessment commentary, confirms our suspicion that faculty are behaving like collaborative learners as they grope toward comfort with new ways of doing old tasks and inventing new tasks to accomplish wholly new ends.

Some Early Indicators of Success

How far and in what ways is revitalization on the Brooklyn campus proceeding? Assessment after the first year indicates that ideas are germinating

among the first thirty-five participants, most of them senior faculty. Presented at seminars and public forums, their ideas reverbate on a campus where an additional thirty-five instructors are preparing OS syllabi, and where yet another eight honors colleagues are working on the course cluster. Out of a total full-time faculty of just over two hundred, informal interaction among so many speaking the same academic language has a powerful impact on daily life. Crossing social, disciplinary, and political lines has produced far more faculty cohesion than could have been predicted for so disparate a professional group.

The objective of improving retention is being realized. Overall retention of entering freshmen has gradually risen, from a low of 43 percent of entering freshmen in 1987 to 65.5 percent in 1991. Judged against a national undergraduate retention average of 70 percent, this evidence confirms that the board's largesse in supporting faculty development and coordinated programming has not been abused. Furthermore, these figures imply that OS and advising strategies are effective means to building community alliances among students, between faculty and students, and even among faculty themselves.

Admissions personnel argue that satisfied freshmen are the best marketing device available to colleges. Equally significant as retention statistics, then, are rising admissions numbers, which for 1992 show an increase of 23 percent. If Noel and Levitz (Noel, Levitz, Saluri, and Associates, 1985, pp. 56–57) are accurate in their assertions about the crucial effect of successful acculturation strategies in retaining students, and if our admissions people are right to cite freshman retention as a predictor of growth, then statistical evidence so far is on the side of positive outcomes.

One unintended outcome of convergent development efforts is that new proposals are spinning off the pilot projects sooner than hoped. The NEH cultural diversity grant has been confirmed. Applicants for next year's continuing grants, both to USDE Title III and to Pew, indicate that departmental alliances have been forged that will result in more course clusters, including some that will connect fields not hitherto linked on this campus, such as science and social science. Indeed, except for the honors program, there has been no effort to mount cross-disciplinary courses for the general curriculum before, and some reluctance even to consider the possibility.

Another unintended outcome is increased curiosity about curricular projects elsewhere. The occasional presence on campus of consultants has created ferment. Visitors report universally positive response to their presence. Whereas two years ago it was difficult to sponsor teams for meetings or institutes, faculty encouraged by their exposure and by response to their formal reports are beginning to volunteer to travel.

Where once only honors courses utilized well-designed field explorations, science and social science departments are beginning to use grant

money to commission faculty experts, including retired colleagues, to help shape student assignments. Of more than passing interest, this process helps to intensify student engagement in learning. Small-group work especially thrives on this kind of immersion in self-guided inquiry, and promotes the goal of peer attachment to which OS has been dedicated.

Response to newsletters, ranging from OS publications featuring student voices to *Connections,* which features short articles by faculty development project participants, has been strong. Readers comment, in fact, that the latter is less a newsletter than a "substantive" minijournal, and have welcomed it enthusiastically.

Finally, an unanticipated outcome of the structure, design, implementation, and initial success of these conjoined efforts is that faculty have begun to see applications for problem-setting approaches to real-life situations—their own. Linking form to function, as an educational objective from which a coherent learning experience grows for students, encourages them to reach for understanding. It helps them to grasp the distinction between understanding and acquiring information, and to see that the latter signifies only if it leads to the former. When faculty are themselves engaged in projects that link form to function, they begin to know—in the deepest and fullest sense of the word—what it is like for their students to learn that way.

Reflections on Lessons Learned

Some of the felt excitement of this year must derive from the uses to which local expertise has been put both to formulate and to implement the convergent development projects that are the subject of this case-study-in-process. Convergence works only when effective partnerships are in place and lines of communication genuinely connect parallel efforts to promote synergistic interactions. Here the most important factors have been faculty-administrative coalition building and organizational flexibility in adapting models for intervention. The latter has capitalized on successful indigenous models that incorporate interactive teaching, cross-disciplinary, and active learning strategies. Both factors turn on involving seasoned practitioners in the honors program and the newer OS.

Faculty-Administrative Coalition Building. Identifying faculty and administrators who might carry out the central mandate to address "the retention problem" is a key factor stimulating vigorous commitment to faculty development. Members of the curriculum committee and pertinent committees of the faculty senate, along with the deans of all governance units, were involved from the outset, and brought into discussions by the provost, who convenes regular meetings of the council of deans on issues and project updates. A general perception is that funded projects rest firmly on positive reaction won by imaginative and persuasive task force reports to the board

during the initial stages of reorganization. The board's support thus became an endorsement of increased retention efforts, campus revitalization, and ultimately of local responsibility for local decisions.

There is a quid pro quo in all this: the senior faculty, however reluctantly, committed itself to redressing attrition by risking its equanimity and privacy. In return for this commitment, the board, however nervously in view of 1987 attrition statistics, risked its standing by providing seed money, without which nothing could have been initiated, and continues to react favorably to faculty development buoyed by the constant increase in retention over the past four years. Continuing-student registration has been rising, with boosts of 8, 12, and 19 percent in the last three years. New students, also on the rise, are up 23 percent this year alone. Combined statistics show an overall student increase of more than 50 percent in the past three years, a record calculated to quicken the heartbeat of any board member.

What in retrospect seems pure serendipity might instead be the result of the care taken to seize upon the elements of an actual situation (largely senior faculty, highly diverse and needy population, pockets of expertise, new organizational structure, poor lines of communication) and bring them into a functional relationship that might yield enterprising results. Task forces and planning committees all involved both faculty and administration. Once three grants were underway, the emerging resource room came to symbolize synergism once it was opened to all faculty development groups. A coordinating committee, on which project directors from all grants sit, appointed itself and now sponsors a newsletter, *Connections,* to which all participants may submit entries. This joint group organized a faculty workshop to inaugurate the 1992–93 academic year: "Teaching and Learning—Some Practical & Interactive Approaches to Enhancing the Classroom Experience." In such an atmosphere, it is no accident that the codirector of the honors program thought fit to apply for an NEH grant to support study of non-Western texts suitable for undergraduates. This fourth development project begins while others are in their second year, and can only add to the synergism of the overall convergent project model.

Organizational Flexibility. The sense of genuine possibilities and options has brought about these possibilities and options. But sense alone does not produce results. The third structural factor for persistent growth is flexibility. For people to take part in programs, courses, projects, and activities that make them feel like students again, which is semitraumatic for some, room to maneuver is necessary.

In this setting it has come from several quarters: from administrator partners; from the faculty senate, whose leadership saw a need for significant measures of campus autonomy to create real change; and very importantly, from the faculty union. Once the provost invited union representatives to participate in her dean's council meetings, a mechanism existed to participate more meaningfully in faculty development generally. These representatives

are among the grant-funded initial cohorts, even coordinating funded projects in some cases. Union leaders are therefore both liaisons and spokespeople. As such they are parties responsible for the outcome of curricular innovation and professional mastery.

One happy coincidence in this year of convergence is that negotiations for a new contract made it possible for union leaders to bargain for a category of faculty released time reserved for engaging in faculty development. In addition, then, to an already existing pool of released time to support scholarly research, there is now a second pool for development projects as such. This is a tacit acknowledgment that attending to teaching is worthy of support, recognition, and reward. It is also a clear testament to an emerging faculty stake in its own academic revitalization—and a sign that augurs well for the academic future of the Brooklyn campus.

References

Braid, B. "Field-Based Education in 'Semesters.' " *Thought and Action*, 1990, *6*, 93–105.
Noel, L., Levitz, R., Saluri, D., and Associates. *Increasing Student Retention: Effective Programs and Practices for Reducing the Dropout Rate.* San Francisco: Jossey-Bass, 1985.

BERNICE BRAID is professor of comparative literature and dean of academic and instructional resources at Long Island University, Brooklyn Campus, New York.

With support from the Fund for the Improvement of Postsecondary Education (FIPSE), a major research university has developed a program that increases the senior faculty's involvement in undergraduate instruction.

Redefining the Role of Senior Faculty at a Research University

William K. Jackson, Ronald D. Simpson

A prominent leader of a national higher education organization (Knapp, 1990) once noted that the concept of a university where undergraduates are in the presence of faculty working at the frontiers of their fields sometimes seems to mean little more than that the two groups are in the same city. Traditionally, the seniority of faculty members at research universities can be measured by their separation from lower-level undergraduate instruction. Madeleine Green (1990), vice president of the American Council on Education, has commented on the importance of symbolic leadership to the promotion of good teaching. The absence of senior faculty from lower-level undergraduate classes is symbolic of the lack of value assigned by many institutions to that level of instruction.

The University of Georgia in Athens (UGA) is a Carnegie classification Research I university and serves as the flagship institution for the university system of Georgia. The university enrolls over 28,000 students, about 21,000 undergraduates and 7,000 graduate and professional students, and employs approximately 1,850 full-time, tenure-track faculty members. During the late 1960s the university dramatically increased the emphasis placed on research. In recent years UGA has emerged as one of the leading research institutions in the United States.

One indicator of the research emphasis at UGA is the way in which senior faculty budget their time. In the most recent edition of the university's *Fact Book* (Jones, 1991), faculty members at the rank of professor reported spending an average of 3.5 percent of their time on lower-division undergraduate instruction, 8.8 percent on upper-division undergraduate instruction, and

NEW DIRECTIONS FOR TEACHING AND LEARNING, no. 55, Fall 1993   © Jossey-Bass Publishers

20.1 percent on graduate/professional instruction. In contrast, assistant professors reported allocating almost three times as much time to lower-division instruction, and more than twice as much to upper-division undergraduate instruction as did their senior colleagues. Instructors and graduate teaching assistants, by contrast, spent most of their time teaching undergraduates. In *Scholarship Reconsidered: Priorities of the Professoriate* Ernest Boyer (1990) noted that the priorities in American higher education in recent decades have shifted from undergraduate education to graduate education and research. This shift is evident when the duties of the senior faculty at UGA are examined.

In an effort to increase the involvement of senior faculty members in undergraduate instruction at UGA, the Office of Instructional Development (OID) designed a teaching fellows program for senior faculty. Funded by a grant from the Fund for the Improvement of Postsecondary Education (FIPSE), the UGA Senior Teaching Fellows Program was established in the fall of 1988; after three years of FIPSE funding the program became a line item in the UGA budget. Each year this program engages eight senior faculty members in a variety of activities, focusing on numerous topics relevant to teaching, career development, and scholarship.

The specific goals of the Senior Teaching Fellows Program are outlined in the following paragraphs. Details regarding the implementation and outcomes of the program are discussed in subsequent sections of this chapter.

Goals of the Senior Teaching Fellows Program

The major goals of the Senior Teaching Fellows (STF) Program are to improve the quality of teaching and learning at the undergraduate level, to enhance the prestige of undergraduate teaching, and to provide opportunities for renewal for senior faculty. These goals have remained unchanged since the beginning of the program.

The STF program improves the quality of teaching and learning at the undergraduate level in several ways. Each fellow selects an undergraduate course or course sequence that will be the focus of an individual instructional improvement project. Usually, the fellow assumes responsibility for teaching this course or course sequence. For some projects, fellows have mentored teaching assistants or junior faculty who have the responsibility for teaching the project course. In any case, one of the central themes of the STF program is to use the wealth of knowledge and experience of the senior faculty member to enhance instruction in courses that have received little attention from the senior faculty in the past.

The STF program also provides opportunities for the fellows to acquire additional knowledge and skills related to their roles as teachers. Most senior faculty members have never taken education courses or participated in teaching assistant (TA) training programs like those available to graduate students

today. In group meetings held throughout the year the fellows are introduced to instructional concepts that broaden their perspectives as teachers. Topics addressed in these sessions include managing classroom discussion, elements of good test construction, using the case method of teaching, enhancing the multicultural classroom, and effective uses of instructional technologies. The fellows also have opportunities to discuss their individual projects with one another and to examine methods of assessing the effectiveness of their projects in improving teaching and learning.

At the institutional level, the fellows group has emerged as a significant voice for instructional excellence. The president and chief academic officer of the university have, on a number of occasions, used the fellows as a "sounding board" for important new instructional initiatives. The instructional leadership provided by this influential group of distinguished senior faculty has not only stimulated greater efforts toward teaching excellence across the campus but has elevated the prestige associated with undergraduate teaching to a level that more nearly approximates that associated with research productivity.

In order for the STF program to have a significant impact on the prestige assigned to teaching within the culture of the institution, an important condition had to be met. The program had to attract faculty who were not only senior in rank but who were also campus opinion leaders. If the program had been viewed as attracting only those who have ceased to be productive scholars, it would have been a failure. Just recently a current fellow confessed, "When I saw the list of people who had previously been in the program, there was no way I could not accept the invitation to join."

Program Implementation

The establishment of the STF program was facilitated by the existence of a successful Lilly Teaching Fellows program for junior faculty at UGA (Simpson and Jackson, 1990). The Lilly program, also coordinated by OID, provided a model for the design of the STF program. The success of this program for junior faculty members, as well as the university's willingness to continue it after the Lilly Endowment grant ended, demonstrated UGA's ability to implement and sustain high quality faculty development initiatives. In addition, the involvement of senior professors as mentors for the junior faculty members participating in the Lilly program created a high level of interest in a similar program for the senior faculty. The initial proposal to establish the STF program was reviewed and endorsed by a committee of senior faculty members representing all of the university's schools and colleges. During this process several of the institution's most respected senior professors expressed a desire to participate in the program.

The STF program has remained essentially unchanged since 1988 when the first group of senior teaching fellows was selected. Each spring, eight

senior faculty members are selected to participate in a yearlong program beginning the following September. For the first two years of the program, this selection was made by a committee comprised of the current and former chairs of the university-wide committee appointed by the vice president for academic affairs to advise OID. This selection committee has now evolved to include a representative from each group of fellows.

The nature of each year's group of participants is one of the keys to the program's success. Each group represents a wide variety of disciplines. For example, the eight 1991–1992 fellows were drawn from physics, law, comparative literature, music, foods and nutrition, management science, zoology, and language education. In addition, those selected for this program are among the most highly respected senior faculty in the university and most have achieved significant national and international recognition in their disciplines.

A formal application is not required for selection to the program. The names of all senior faculty members who have expressed interest in the program or who have been recommended by other senior colleagues form a list of candidates reviewed by the selection committee. Those selected for the program are contacted to confirm their interest and availability. At that time each participant's department head is asked to pledge approximately 20 percent release time as the department's contribution to the program. All senior faculty members who have been invited to participate in the program have accepted unless prior commitments made participation impossible. The selection committee chooses one or two alternates each year to accommodate this situation.

Once selected, the eight fellows participate in a yearlong series of group and individual activities beginning with a two-day retreat held at a state park in the Georgia mountains at the beginning of the school year. Each fellow receives a grant of $2,500 for an individual instructional improvement project of his or her choice, and they are asked to share their preliminary plans for those projects at this retreat. The retreat also provides the fellows with an opportunity to identify topics to be addressed in group meetings held approximately every two weeks during the academic year. One of the most important aspects of this retreat, and another key to the success of this program, is the opportunity for fellows to become better acquainted. Given the size of the university and the diversity of each group, it is unusual for many of the fellows to know one another very well. Prior to participation in this program, some knew each other only by reputation or through participation on university committees.

During the academic year the fellows meet as a group approximately biweekly in order to discuss important instructional topics. These meetings are normally scheduled in the early evening and include dinner. Typically, a meeting starts at 5:00 P.M. with a presentation by a guest speaker and subsequent discussion. Dinner is served at 6:30 P.M., and informal discussion of the

evening's topic continues during the meal. A dinner meeting will typically conclude by around 8:00 P.M. Many of the topics and speakers for these biweekly meetings are identified by the group at the beginning-of-the-year retreat. Other topics are suggested by the program staff or individual fellows as the year progresses. In addition, several of these biweekly meetings are reserved for discussion of the fellows' individual projects.

Each group of fellows meets at least once with the university's president and vice president for academic affairs. These administrators use these occasions to seek advice from the fellows on important instructional issues. At one such meeting the vice president for academic affairs asked the group to react to a plan for enhancing the university's teaching awards program. In meetings with the president, the fellows groups have been asked to recommend actions to advance instruction at the university.

A second two-day retreat is held each year in May. At this meeting the fellows reflect on their experience during the year, make recommendations for the program for the following year, and discuss potential candidates for the program. The group also discusses ways of continuing their involvement in the program following their fellowship year. Several group projects have emerged from this retreat, including a university-wide conference on teaching and a plan for quarterly meetings that would include all former as well as current fellows. Following this retreat, the fellows continue to work on their individual projects and a committee is formed to select the next group.

Program Outcomes

One of the most difficult things to accomplish with any faculty development program is evaluation. Most often we evaluate those things easiest to see or count while overlooking the more hard-to-measure phenomena. Sometimes the latent, less obvious outcomes end up being the most significant over the long term. So evaluation of the STF program continues, and it will be years before the complete impact of the program can be assessed.

Meanwhile, we have focused primarily on the goals of the program for short-term assessment and feedback. The fellows supply evidence of impact relative to the projects they conduct. They also give us both quantitative and anecdotal information on how well they think the goals of the program are being met. In addition, the program codirectors are able to provide data from senior administrators and other university-level sources. The combination of multilevel, multimethod approaches over time has provided rich formative as well as summative information. Outcomes relating to each of the program goals are presented next.

Improving the Quality of Undergraduate Teaching and Learning. Several fellows have taken pre- and postintervention measures in an attempt to measure increases in learning as a result of their instructional projects. The comments of a professor of management were not uncommon. He stated in

response to evaluations of his multimedia project, "My overall effectiveness scores on student evaluation were the highest I have ever received." Several other faculty members experienced similar results as they compared student evaluations with past quarters.

Three participants in the first year of the program used outside expert evaluators. A fellow in genetics and a fellow in comparative literature utilized services of the Office of Instructional Development to evaluate their jointly taught interdisciplinary course, "Science and Humanities: The Two Cultures." All indicators used by the expert evaluator pointed to the fact that this course was one of a kind and that endeavors like this are both desirable and possible on the UGA campus.

Peer evaluation and involvement is another method used to assess instructional effectiveness. One senior teaching fellow in evaluating his instructional project commented, "The single most important outcome of this project was the acceptance of this method of instruction by other faculty members in my department." In this case, the leadership of one faculty member in pioneering self-paced, individualized instruction influenced an entire academic unit. In another case, one of the fellows was acknowledged by the dean of Arts and Sciences in a campuswide publication for "distinguished service to his field and continuing his commitment to quality instruction."

A fellow in romance languages developed a training program for TAs in her department and brought to the campus two highly acclaimed experts in Portuguese to evaluate her project. Their feedback indicated that this fellow's program was at the leading edge of her field in the country. Through these initial endeavors have emerged several other activities and programs for enhancement of teaching by TAs in the Department of Romance Languages at the University of Georgia.

When one shifts the focus from teaching to learning, evaluation becomes even more complex. All participants are encouraged to evaluate student learning outcomes and, where possible, make pre- and postproject comparisons. The following account written by a professor of political science points out the difficulty of evaluating this aspect of our first goal:

> At this time I only have preliminary evaluations of my efforts to restructure an introductory course to realize higher order learning objectives. I am scheduled to team-teach the same course next Spring, so I will be able to start to collect student assessments and also to compare student performance measures. I am planning to follow the criminal justice majors who completed the course in question [that is, those in the spring 1991 semester] and to track their progress in our program of study. Specifically, I plan to study their performance in the courses required of all majors and their completion of the analytical logs and senior thesis that all majors are required to complete in their 15-credit internships. This will take some time (1–2 years) but it will enable me to see if the students who have taken the

restructured introductory course in 1991 and 1992 are better able to complete central major requirements in a fashion superior to students who enrolled in the past.

Another fellow who developed supplementary materials for a large management course enrolling five hundred students reported: "Student performance appeared to improve. In a class where, historically, half the students earn grades above 'C,' with a numerical average of approximate 76, my class average this past winter quarter (the first real test of my new materials [slides and transparencies]) was just over 80."

Two faculty reported, as a result of their projects and of the many ideas they had gained from their involvement in the program, that significant increases in student enrollments had resulted. As one of these persons put it, "Something must be happening in the lower levels to motivate students to continue in our classes."

In effect, there are numerous indicators that learning is being enhanced through this program. The overall positive impact of the senior teaching fellows at the University of Georgia is so clear in so many ways that fine-tuned quantitative measures hardly appear necessary. Yet, with the documented accomplishments of the specific goals of the program will come excellent opportunities for further research and continued assessment of this faculty development activity.

In every fellow's instructional improvement project evaluated during the first three years there was evidence that improvement in the quality of undergraduate teaching and learning had occurred. These indicators were both individual and group in nature. In other words, it was possible to see improvement in specific courses as well as improvement at the departmental and college level.

Improving the Credibility of Undergraduate Teaching on Campus. The following quote by a distinguished geneticist and member of the National Academy of Sciences speaks to the accomplishment of the second goal of the STF program: "During the past 10 years, my teaching has been almost entirely in graduate courses. The 'Science and Literature' course gave me a new appreciation of the rewards of teaching undergraduates, and one result is that I have volunteered to teach in our new introductory biology course for science majors. I am developing both classroom sessions and lab exercises for this course now, and I am relying heavily on what I learned during the FIPSE Senior Fellows program." In fact, the participation of this faculty member during the first year of the program was instrumental in attracting other superior faculty members in subsequent years. Another professor in physics, through his project, was able to get additional time from his department head for working with his laboratory instruction project. He was also able to get more TAs assigned to the project. In this case, the importance of instruction was elevated in a department with a long tradition of a strong research emphasis.

The manner in which the STF program has enhanced the credibility of undergraduate teaching at the University of Georgia is perhaps best summarized by a professor of mathematics:

> My participation in the 1990–91 Senior Fellows program afforded me the opportunity to shape the essential pieces of a far-reaching plan whose underlying theme is the use of computational technology to energize the teaching of mathematics at The University of Georgia. If these different pieces can be brought together successfully, the result may well be a significant enhancement of the mathematics learning experiences of thousands of University undergraduates. I believe that, when we look back a few years hence, it will be clear to all that this program played a unique and pivotal role in the rededication of The University of Georgia to its primary mission of undergraduate teaching and learning.

Several senior teaching fellows have won prestigious awards during or after participating in the program. In a number of cases the individuals attributed their recognition directly to their involvement in this program. Two participants were promoted from associate professor to professor the year after their participation. These faculty members felt that the visibility and credibility of this program helped them in their efforts to be recognized as good scholars in their fields. Another participant was named a university professor the year after his participation. Two participants from the first year are now heads of their departments, a third has become an associate dean, and a fourth was recently appointed dean of the university's largest college. Eight fellows have now won the Josiah Meigs Award for Excellence in Teaching, the highest award for excellence in teaching given by the University of Georgia.

Several prominent and visible curriculum changes are direct results of this program. A major new program in Japanese studies was assisted and has now emerged as a new degree program; the introductory course in political science was restructured; a major revamping of a laboratory manual in geology was accomplished; four Portuguese courses were completely revised; new syllabi for TA training programs were written; a workshop on critical thinking was conducted; a major curriculum change is underway in the School of Forest Resources; a course in child and family development was revamped; and one fellow presented his project on interactive videodisc technology to a national meeting in his discipline.

On several occasions the president and vice president for academic affairs have called on the fellows for discussion and advice on campuswide issues. One such occasion led to a university-wide symposium on the topic of balancing teaching and research. Several fellows were involved in a major revision of promotion and tenure guidelines. Also, several senior teaching fellows have served on the president's advisory committee, and for the past

two years a fellow has served as chair of the executive committee of the university council, the faculty governance body at UGA. In all of these activities, the general outcome has been that teaching has gained additional support and has reached a healthier balance with research as a valued enterprise on campus.

Providing Opportunities for Professional Renewal for Senior Faculty. Without exception, the fellows who participated in this program felt that it added a dimension of renewal and revitalization to their academic and social lives. One highly respected senior faculty member's statement summarizes what was consistently felt by participants: "This past year as a Senior Fellow has been one of the high points of my teaching career."

The most significant factor in this program is the interpersonal ties that form during the year of participation and afterward. One faculty member remarked two years after he had participated that the program had been the most renewing experience of his entire career.

Another way in which participants engage in professional renewal is through their projects. In almost all cases the projects provide opportunities for additional growth and stimulation. Travel, interaction with outside experts, relevant conferences, new courses, new methods of instruction, and the addition of new ideas to established courses are mentioned as prime sources of renewal. The fellows are unanimous in this regard and repeatedly cite examples of how their direct experiences in the program led to self-renewal and revitalization.

A major outcome of this program has been the achievement of this third goal. Hard-working, high-powered scholars need time for reflection, socializing, and self-actualization. The Senior Teaching Fellows program provided this in large doses. Perhaps the best indicator of how important this program has become in the lives of its participants is their spontaneous and unanimous desire to continue meeting as a full group. Last year in addition to the new participants meeting twice a month, the full group met quarterly to hear outstanding speakers or discuss with the vice president for academic affairs important campuswide issues. During the spring meeting they presented the vice president for academic affairs and the program codirectors honorary memberships as senior teaching fellows.

All fellows from the first four years are adamant regarding their belief in the value of the program. The program directors continue to hear comments on a weekly basis, such as, "This program has been one of the major highlights of my entire career," and "I cannot tell you the boost I have received from the special way in which we are treated in the program." Now that the momentum is going and the program is moving ahead with funding by the university, there will be a continuation of the many remarkable outcomes described in this chapter. Not only are students likely to continue learning more, the culture at the university is changing and teaching is moving up the ladder of importance as a valued activity for all of the faculty.

Reflections and Implications

What has been learned from this program, and what is needed to launch and sustain such an activity for senior faculty? A major lesson learned is that senior faculty need opportunities for change and renewal. By showing them that their institution cares, by going that extra mile to treat them specially, great dividends can accrue with surprisingly small amounts of funding. The opportunity to exchange ideas with colleagues from across campus, the formation of a support group, and the ability to delve into instructional topics (often for the first time) are examples of things that senior faculty desire and appreciate when made available.

Key factors to consider in establishing and maintaining such a faculty development program are: (1) make it an honor to be a participant; (2) marshal support from the top; (3) select participants who have something to bring to the program and who can work well together as a group; and (4) give the participants freedom to help set the agenda and steer the program. If the first two or three years attract high-caliber people and they find the activities beneficial, they will sell the program. Like most things in the academy, credibility and reputation are critical.

Regardless of the size or type of institution, an initiative like the Senior Teaching Fellows program at the University of Georgia will likely succeed anywhere if planned for and nurtured properly. The keys are thoughtful planning, developing trust and esprit de corps, strong staff support, and strong leadership from faculty members who participate. It is also important to carefully consider the history, structure, and unique culture of a campus and allow for flexibility and creativity as the local program emerges. In essence, if the program is designed primarily with those it serves in mind, it will succeed. It will also lead to a greater sense of community within the institution and generate many exciting outcomes that cannot be imagined.

References

Boyer, E. L. *Scholarship Reconsidered: Priorities of the Professoriate.* Princeton, N.J.: Carnegie Foundation for the Advancement of Teaching, 1990.

Green, M. F. "Why Good Teaching Needs Active Leadership." In P. Seldin and Associates, *How Administrators Can Improve Teaching: Moving from Talk to Action in Higher Education.* San Francisco: Jossey-Bass, 1990.

Jones, L. G. (ed.). *The University of Georgia Fact Book 1991.* Athens: University of Georgia Press, 1991.

Knapp, C. B. "State of the University Address." *Columns,* Nov. 12, 1990, p. 4.

Simpson, R. D., and Jackson, W. K. "A Multidimensional Approach to Faculty Vitality: The University of Georgia." In J. H. Schuster, D. W. Wheeler, and Associates, *Enhancing Faculty Careers: Strategies for Development and Renewal.* San Francisco: Jossey-Bass, 1990.

WILLIAM K. JACKSON is a career academic administrator who serves as associate director of the Office of Instructional Development at the University of Georgia.

RONALD D. SIMPSON is professor of science education and higher education and director of the Office of Instructional Development at the University of Georgia.

Two states, New Jersey and Washington, have developed novel approaches to supporting faculty development. Particular programs in each state have brought faculty members—including many senior faculty—to work together in new ways to revitalize their teaching and the experience of teaching.

Revitalizing Senior Faculty Through Statewide Efforts

Barbara Leigh Smith, Myrna J. Smith

As large numbers of faculty approach retirement age and new teachers enter the academy, the face of American colleges and universities will change. Maintaining the vitality of the entire teaching corps and building bridges between the generations are critical elements in maintaining healthy academic communities. Addressing the needs and interests of senior faculty is a significant component of this endeavor. Of course, the category "senior faculty" covers a broad, diverse group of people, and effective faculty development programs should recognize this diversity. Some senior faculty complain about isolation and the lack of challenge in their work environment. Others feel the absence of any sense of community. Some older faculty express a feeling of becoming more and more marginal as the priorities and issues on their campuses shift. Others feel disgruntled, tired, and cynical about the endless energy drain of college governance and seemingly intractable conflicts.

In regard to teaching, some senior faculty complain about their students' levels of preparation, their lack of motivation, and their narrow backgrounds in terms of cultural information. Faculty point to the increasing size of their classes, and the repetitiveness and mind-deadening redundancy of teaching the same courses over and over again. With great precision, one faculty member told us that she will face 125 more sections of English 101–102 before retirement; another precisely forecast the number of freshman essays she has left to read. In a reflective autobiographical essay, a third wrote about his fear

We are grateful to Jean MacGregor for her helpful comments on an earlier draft of this chapter.

that he "is becoming the kind of faculty member that administrators shudder at getting stuck with; the kind that I shudder at getting stuck with." Another puzzled at the insight that all of the really vital parts of her life took place outside her work environment, and wondered when and why this had happened.

Many senior faculty describe their work and their institutional relations as reaching a certain "plateau" after a number of years, a plateau that becomes a ceiling on subsequent relationships and aspirations. These ceilings take many different forms—defining and limiting what and how we teach as well as our institutional roles and our relationships with others. These ceilings can come to define what is possible, and what is not possible, removing much of the learning, the pleasures, the surprises, and the puzzles from everyday life. They can stifle curiosity—a key ingredient in maintaining intellectual vitality.

Unfortunately, many institutions have relatively narrow notions of what it takes to maintain faculty vitality over the long term. Too little attention is paid to the variety of senior faculty needs. All too often there is a "blame the victim" mentality. Senior faculty are characterized as burned out, withdrawn, and in need of rehabilitation and tune-ups; this chapter, and the institutions and programs described in it, are based on the conviction that this characterization is inaccurate. What senior faculty really need is greater challenges and opportunities.

Too often, institutions—like their faculty members—labor in isolation. Two states, Washington and New Jersey, have invested in statewide centers to provide ongoing structure and sustenance to the higher education community. This chapter describes how state policy can support teaching, learning, and faculty development through statewide efforts, highlighting two specific faculty development approaches that have been particularly successful in engaging senior faculty: the Partners in Learning Program (formerly the New Jersey Master Faculty Program) and the Learning Community effort in Washington State.

Statewide Faculty Development Initiatives in New Jersey

In New Jersey, statewide support for faculty development comes from two sources: the New Jersey Department of Higher Education (NJDHE) and the New Jersey Institute for Collegiate Teaching and Learning (NJICTL), founded by the NJDHE in 1989. NJDHE has supported faculty development programs on individual public and private campuses by means of competitive grants and specialized programs such as writing across the curriculum, internationalizing the curriculum, retention, and gender projects. NJICTL sponsors faculty development programs, works with faculty to promote disciplinary reform, and conducts research; in all these efforts, NJICTL works with both public and private campuses. Some of its initiatives include an annual Faculty College, a Faculty Development Network, Curriculum En-

hancement Conferences, and the Partners in Learning Program (Smith, Golin, and Friedman, 1992).

Origins of the New Jersey Institute. The New Jersey Institute for Collegiate Teaching and Learning was established by state contract at Seton Hall University by the New Jersey Department of Higher Education in 1989 in order to support faculty development across all sectors of higher education in the state. Previously existing programs such as the New Jersey Master Faculty Program (now Partners in Learning), the Faculty Development Network, and Curriculum Enhancement Conferences were moved to NJICTL. Other programs, including a Faculty Fellow-in-Residence and the Faculty College, were added. The research projects, including one on senior faculty, discussed elsewhere in this volume, emerged from and supported the further development of these programs, especially Partners in Learning. In the first three years of NJICTL's existence several hundred faculty from forty-three campuses attended its programs. Senior faculty have participated and profited greatly, particularly through participation in the Partners in Learning Program.

Partners in Learning Program. Partners in Learning, developed in the 1980s by the late Joseph Katz, is a simple but comprehensive faculty development program that has engaged faculty from many colleges and universities in New Jersey, Kansas, Pennsylvania, Louisiana, Connecticut, Missouri, and other states. Involving faculty both intellectually and emotionally, this program reinvigorates them and encourages them to reflect on their own teaching. (For descriptions of the program, see Katz and Henry, 1988; Golin, 1990; Smith and LaCelle-Peterson, 1991; Smith, Golin, and Friedman, 1992.)

The program focuses on the question "How do students learn?," and promotes faculty collaboration through classroom observation, student interviews, and collegial discussion. Golin (1990) points out its four strengths: it is ongoing, faculty-owned, decentralized, and transforming. Another strength is its flexibility, which makes Partners in Learning travel well—so well that single campuses, college and university systems, and consortia of institutions across the country have adopted the program. Although teaching is the main activity of most faculty in higher education, it is often the least collegial, most isolated, part of their work. This isolation, tolerable at age thirty, becomes deadening by age fifty. Each of the three essential components of the program works to make teaching less isolating, more collegial.

Classroom Observation. The basic unit of the program is the faculty pair. One partner observes a class taught by the other, for a semester, quarter, or any agreed-upon time period. During the next semester or other time period they switch roles. How often these observations take place depends upon the pair themselves. The more frequent the observation, the more involved the observer becomes in the class. Katz and Henry (1988) recommend a weekly observation; however, many faculty find that time constraints limit their observations to every other week. That the observer become familiar with the

content, the students, the assignments, the evaluation, as well as the teacher, is what really matters.

Katz and Henry (1988) suggested that the pairs should be from different disciplines so that the observations and discussions can focus on teaching and learning. However, some participants around the country have indicated particular interest in seeing a colleague teach familiar subject matter and have paired within their disciplines without negative results. Senior faculty, although they appreciate guidelines about pairing and other aspects of the program, will adapt the program to their own satisfaction.

Student Interviews. Each of the partners interviews two or three students from the observed class several times over the period of class observation. Although the one-on-one interview has been the primary form of obtaining responses from students, faculty have conducted variations, including both partners interviewing one to three students; either partner interviewing two or three students; and the observer interviewing the entire class. All methods yield information useful to learning about how students learn. Written responses from students might also provide the necessary information, but what makes the interviews powerful is the emotional component. And that emotional component contributes to faculty change.

The advantage of interviewing individual students over the course of a quarter or a semester is that it allows a faculty member to follow a student's perception over time. Moreover, if the trust level develops as it should, students will speak more openly after several interviews. Students, who might be reticent to say anything negative about the class or reveal any personal difficulties, become more willing to speak honestly once they determine that the faculty member wants a sincere dialogue. Students can be selected in a variety of ways: some faculty ask for volunteers; others look for diversity in race, class, age, gender, and sexual orientation; others select students by their academic performance. Some faculty at Southeast Missouri State selected students on the basis of their learning styles as determined by the Meyers-Briggs test (personal interview with Renee Betz, Apr. 1992).

The student interviews usually begin with general questions and move to more specific ones. A faculty member might begin with, "Why are you attending this college?" and "What are your goals?" in a first interview, and progress to such questions as, "What did you learn in the lab on Tuesday?" and "At any point were you bored in Monday's class?" All faculty members need to develop their own questions as they evolve out of the material and the personalities of the focal class. Students generally respond positively to being interviewed. One student commented, "This is the first time a teacher asked for my opinion about classes." Others are pleased to be a part of a project about improving teaching.

Collegial Discussion. Participants at a campus meet regularly to discuss the observations and interviews. Because these meetings are based on the direct experience of faculty involved in the program, less posturing and more

dialogue generally occurs. Some participants have reported that the meetings are the most valuable part of the program. Palmer (1992, p. 12) notes in his essay on reform of teaching and learning that the second stage of any reform movement takes place when isolated individuals "discover each other and form groups for mutual support." Senior faculty meeting just to talk about their experiences with teaching, or observing teaching, or interviewing students would fit his category, especially when done on an informal basis.

Most programs across the country have been organized with administrative support. The three components of the program require considerable coordination to help faculty find partners, to organize campus meetings, and to represent the program to the administration (particularly if they involve requests for money). For that reason, most campuses around the country have selected one or sometimes two campus coordinators. (For a detailed description on starting a program, see New Jersey Institute for Collegiate Teaching and Learning, 1991.)

What Is Accomplished Through Partners in Learning? A three-year study to document the impact of the program on the students of faculty participants is just beginning; evidence that Partners in Learning is a successful program for faculty, however, comes from several sources. First, the program was formally evaluated by R. Eugene Rice and Sandra I. Cheldelin (1989) in a report entitled "The Knower and the Known: Making the Connection." Second, a selection of 254 essays written by faculty who participated during the first three years of the project was published in *Essays by Coordinators and Participants in the New Jersey Master Faculty Program* (1990), edited by Patricia Morrissey. Third, NJICTL staff conducted an informal series of interviews with selected participants to see how their teaching or their feeling about teaching had changed as a result of participation in Partners in Learning.

Rice and Cheldelin (1989) found that faculty (1) developed greater awareness of differences in students' levels of preparation and developmental stages; (2) broadened their repertoire of teaching techniques and became more purposeful in employing them; and (3) found new enthusiasm for the practice of teaching. Austin and Baldwin (1992, p. 41) point out that, whether faculty are team teaching, working together to teach a cluster of courses, or involved in peer observation or student interviews, three benefits occur when faculty collaborate: "development of their teaching ability, new intellectual stimulation, and a closer connection to the university or college as a community." All of these have occurred with Partners in Learning, but some are easier to document than others.

Follow-up interviews confirm Rice and Cheldelin's first conclusion: a broadened sensitivity to the needs of students. Many faculty became aware of their students' personal and family problems as well as their lack of academic preparedness. One professor of nursing at a private, liberal arts college, who participated in Partners in Learning for three years, became aware that

beginning nursing students did not have the academic skills necessary to succeed in their program. Working with a colleague in academic foundations, she initiated a lab component to the introductory nursing program. The content of the course was essentially study skills, but since the skills applied directly to an essential major course, she believed it was more meaningful to students. In this case the greater awareness of differences in students' level of preparedness led to action.

Faculty who participate in the program continue to broaden their repertoire of teaching techniques; hopefully that also means they develop their teaching abilities. Most of these "newly discovered" techniques require the student to participate more actively in their own learning. Faculty who have observed other classes over time and who have interviewed students discover that students want to be involved in the class and prefer classes where teachers don't "just lecture." A business education professor who had relied almost exclusively on lectures now uses more student groups, simulations, and projects. A theoretical physics teacher took a vow never to do another problem on the board for students; he decided to let them do the problems and to help each other with the solutions. Two math teachers, who have participated for two years, have students sit in cooperative groups so that switching from teacher explanation to student problem solving can be done throughout the class.

The easiest point to confirm is newfound enthusiasm. Faculty members offered many positive appraisals:

> The Program can get you out of the rut—going to class, presenting prepared material, giving exams, grading them, reading papers. It makes you think more about teaching, beyond the mechanics of a given class. You can become more experimental, and you have interested faculty members back you up or set you straight. . . . Partners in a great, on-going dialogue on teaching. [New Jersey Institute for Collegiate Teaching and Learning, 1991, p. 9]

> The Partners in Learning Program gives you back more energy than it takes—unlike most everything else faculty do. [New Jersey Institute for Collegiate Teaching and Learning, 1991, p. 15]

This newfound enthusiasm for teaching, along with the collegial discussions, contributes to faculty feeling more a part of the college community.

Follow-up interviews also brought this disturbing, although hardly unexpected news: once participants leave the program the gains they may have made in their teaching may not be permanent. An English professor at a research university wrote in one of her end-of-the-term essays that she was becoming more student-centered, spending more class time on the students' own work, rather than on analyses of the texts. In a follow-up interview, two

years after she had left the program, she was not sure whether she was as student-centered because "I am not talking with anyone about teaching." The nursing professor referred to above noted that she was a backslider, having returned to using considerably more lectures. Because of the outside licensing exam, she wanted to be sure she "covered the material" that would be on the exam. She had no hard evidence that students did better or worse on the state examination depending upon the method of teaching she used, but she felt more comfortable about her responsibility when she relied more on lectures.

These illustrations make us painfully aware of the need for ongoing classroom assessment and student outcome data. Decisions about teaching seem to be made by the professor's own comfort level, rather than by reference to any convincing data. Former participants' experiences also indicate that senior faculty, like graduate students or any other group of faculty, need ongoing dialogue about teaching. Partners in Learning has proven successful in revitalizing faculty mainly because its structure requires dialogue at three levels: with the students, with a peer, and with a group of colleagues. However, the most successful programs of all may be ones that require ongoing curricular reform, such as the learning communities of Washington State.

Educational Reform in Washington State

The state of Washington has been simultaneously pursuing two contrasting approaches to educational improvement: a centralized approach through statewide policy and incentives and a grass-roots approach that is more faculty based and directly linked to teaching and learning. The centralized approach is guided by a Higher Education Coordinating Board and a state master plan that addresses issues such as funding, access, admissions standards, institutional roles and missions, and assessment. Like most states, Washington is trying to improve its educational system in a time of limited resources, and there is special interest in economical approaches that have broad impact.

What is most unique about educational reform in Washington is a grass-roots effort, led by the Washington Center for Improving the Quality of Undergraduate Education. It involves large and growing numbers of faculty and administrators. The center treats curriculum development, faculty development, and institutional change as interrelated issues. It emphasizes long-term issues rather than short-term projects. It concentrates on building enduring relationships, networks, and teams rather than working with random individuals. The Washington Center's eight-year history suggests that its approach is very effective in revitalizing faculty and improving undergraduate education.

Origins of the Washington Center. The idea for the Washington Center dates back to 1984 when two colleges—The Evergreen State College and

Seattle Central Community College—started collaborating on a curricular change initiative (Smith and Hunter, 1988; Smith, 1988). Seattle Central wanted to develop some interdisciplinary programs similar to Evergreen's and asked for assistance. Interinstitutional faculty exchanges and team teaching became the vehicles that enabled faculty from the two institutions to learn from one another. This kind of close interaction between a two-year and a four-year college in Washington was unprecedented. Word about the energy and success of this partnership spread quickly through Washington's community college system. It suggested new possibilities for interinstitutional collaboration, and teachers at other colleges were eager to become involved.

In 1985, with growing grass-roots interest and modest support from the Exxon Foundation and the Ford Foundation, the Washington Center was officially established as a new statewide consortium devoted to improving undergraduate education. Interest in the center's work rapidly spread. In just two years, the consortium had tripled in size and was institutionalized with state funding of approximately $200,000 a year. Headquartered at The Evergreen State College, the Washington Center is now eight years old and serves forty-three institutions, including both two-year and four-year colleges and universities and both public and independent institutions in Washington. Since half of the freshmen in Washington begin their college career in a community college, the avid participation of the state's two-year colleges is especially notable and important.

Learning Communities and Educational Restructuring. The most powerful aspect of the Washington Center's work has been helping faculty and administrators throughout Washington think about ways to restructure the curriculum into "learning communities" to enhance teaching and learning. A variety of different curricular approaches—all commonly referred to as "learning community" models—are being used by the colleges and universities associated with the Washington Center (Gabelnick, MacGregor, Matthews, and Smith, 1990; Smith, 1991). These range from linked courses to the fully integrated team-taught coordinated studies program that characterizes Evergreen's curriculum.

The model used successfully for more than eight years at Seattle Central and at more than a dozen other Washington colleges directly replicates the Evergreen curricular approach. Instead of fulfilling general education requirements by taking a series of disciplinary courses, students enroll in an intensive fifteen to eighteen credit interdisciplinary program, called a "coordinated study program," for one term. This single program is the "full load" for both the faculty and students. Coordinated studies programs typically enroll sixty to eighty students, and three or four faculty plan and teach the program together. Many address broad interdisciplinary questions or themes. Recent coordinated studies programs include such titles as "The Making of Americans: Individualism" (involving political economy, art, lit-

erature, and history); "Power and the Person" (visual art, philosophy, music, and literature); "Science Shakes the Foundations: Perspectives on Marx, Dickens, and Darwin" (political economy, English literature, biology, and history), and "Speaking for Ourselves: Cross-Cultural Visions and Connections" (minority literature, composition, history, non-Western art, and sociology).

The key element of all learning community models is that they restructure the educational environment to provide greater curricular coherence and more intensive interaction between students and faculty. All involve some degree of collaborative planning and/or teaching. Implementing learning communities requires new levels of cross-institutional support to deal with student recruitment, publicity, advising, and registration. The programs bring diverse elements of the college community together, often creating a renewed sense of involvement and common purpose. As a result, they frequently improve the campus climate. They have been especially effective in creating a sense of academic engagement and community on commuter campuses.

In Washington senior faculty have been leaders in the statewide establishment of these learning community programs. The new curricular initiatives first attracted the innovators and risk-takers among the senior faculty, people who were at the forefront of most campus initiatives. They in turn drew in many of their colleagues and friends, who had been hired at the same time and been at the institution for twenty to twenty-five years. The strong presence of highly skilled senior faculty is certainly part of the reason learning communities have been so successful in Washington. These faculty are broadly educated and well trained in their disciplines. They are mature educators with clear educational values, and a strong sense of their own authority. Many of their colleagues relished the opportunity to teach with them. Teachers *do* make a difference, and we need better ways to leverage the talent of gifted teachers. Efforts to recognize and reward exemplary teaching, for example, usually have relatively narrow goals focused on the individual. Learning communities provide one avenue for amplifying talent through the vehicle of team teaching.

Why Restructuring Efforts in Washington State Have Worked. Understanding why learning communities work offers some important clues about faculty development and educational change. Learning communities work because they represent a complex, educationally sound, and practical solution to a complicated set of educational issues. They provide a coordinated response to issues about curriculum reform, staff development, and organizational change. They empower faculty and build community by providing an effective structure for rebuilding dialogue within our institutions.

Faculty who teach in learning communities become deeply engaged with their students and colleagues, and they come to view their disciplines in new

ways. English teachers connecting writing to other general education courses such as art history, American government, or introductory biology become familiar with the unique discourse norms of different disciplines. The teachers from the other disciplines, in turn, gain new perspectives on the intimate connection between thinking, learning, and writing. As they work with colleagues with different disciplinary and pedagogical backgrounds, faculty members have the opportunity to gain new perspectives and to try out new approaches in a relatively risk-free environment. One colleague noted that he would have been afraid to experiment with peer writing groups without a more knowledgeable colleague in the classroom, but after a quarter of working with a teammate he had the confidence to continue using them. Team teaching in learning communities has been an important vehicle for teachers to broaden their pedagogical repertoire.

In learning communities faculty and students are together for substantial amounts of time. Faculty are not simply teaching their old courses back-to-back (in most models). They are planning a coordinated curriculum with their colleagues and looking for intersections as well as differences between their disciplines. The learning community enterprise is intense and intimate. Faculty are working together on a daily basis: planning curriculum, designing and critiquing assignments, discussing and evaluating students. Each day they observe and learn from each other, and this sustained contact continues for a whole quarter or a whole semester, providing invaluable coaching and mentoring. Furthermore, they are working together with a common set of students eight to sixteen hours per week. While multiple authority figures in the classroom can be confusing to some students, team teaching has many advantages in terms of modeling teamwork, providing different points of view, and simply reaching students who have different learning styles and needs.

By concentrating the curriculum and the time spent together, learning communities encourage both faculty and students to vest deeply and to assume more responsibility. In contrast, the typical teaching and learning environment diffuses teaching and learning energy and fragments responsibility. With only a fraction of the student's time, even the most committed teacher feels the frustration of partial commitment. Joseph Tussman (1969) noted this problem, many years ago when he said that students present themselves to the teacher in fragments and not even the advising system can put a student together again. The student is constantly beleaguered by choices: to pursue one thread is to drop another. The student seldom experiences the delight of sustained conversations and instead lives the life of a distracted juggler. Gerald Graff (1990) made the same point more recently, arguing that the problem of curricular reform is primarily an organizational dilemma of too much fragmentation.

Learning communities also rekindle faculty commitment because they offer a profoundly creative arena. By asking the faculty literally to re-create

the curriculum (at least in the more radical forms of learning communities), these programs establish a climate of growth, trust, permission, and personal responsibility—key elements in self-renewal. In a very real sense, learning communities demand that we again become professors who "profess" what we think is worth teaching while providing a coherent and supportive teaching environment. But they let us "profess" in a way that works, through a creative process of curriculum design rather than a process of political negotiation in a curriculum committee. This suggests that faculty vitality and empowerment are critically bound up with questions about the balance between responsibility and control.

The fact that learning communities have been particularly attractive to midcareer faculty suggests a real readiness on their part to assume larger roles. The boredom and tedium that come from the same old roles and teaching the same old courses is an important and neglected issue at many institutions. As one educator who was contemplating her sixteenth year at the same institution put it, "If you don't see new challenges, you get worried about losing your edge." Clearly, learning communities rekindle the creative side of teaching and provide new challenges for well-established teachers. One senior professor remarked that "they work because they turn everyone into a learner again and remind us why we went into this business in the first place." But there are some deeper lessons here. It is also clear that learning communities work because they go beyond the individual and are a basis for coming together to build the "larger educational enterprise." They provide a powerful associative structure in an environment with few effective centripetal forces. Learning communities seem to represent an effective bridge among us, what one professor at North Seattle Community College has called a structure for "authentic dialogue." At the individual level, they help release and leverage new energy by providing an alternative "frame" on what's possible, but they also provide an empowering group structure that works in a way that our more individualistic approaches to faculty development and educational reform often do not. Some years ago Joe Katz (1987, p. 28) noted that "continuous learning on the part of the faculty seems to be a prerequisite for the needed transformation of teaching." We would build on his insight to say, "Associative structures that support continuous learning on the part of groups of faculty seem to be a prerequisite for the needed transformation of our colleges."

In Washington, learning communities have prospered partly because support systems have been built within and across institutions to encourage reflection and ongoing learning. The Washington Center offers an array of additional services to support learning community programs across the state: conferences, consultants, faculty exchanges, publications, seed grants, and assessment support. At the same time, individual campuses are also developing their own innovative ways of supporting the new curriculum initiatives.

Implications for State Support of Faculty Development

As large numbers of new faculty members enter the academy, it is easy to shift institutional focus away from the needs of the professoriate as a whole. Too often, segmentation of the faculty and bifurcation of the community is the result. The experience in both Washington and New Jersey suggests that this need not occur. There are creative and relatively inexpensive ways to build community and increased focus on teaching and learning. It is also clear that many senior faculty have an enormous interest in educational improvement and a thirst for greater collegiality. They respond enthusiastically to opportunities for "authentic dialogue" about teaching and learning and they can provide critically needed leadership for educational reform.

The New Jersey Partners in Learning Program and the learning community effort in Washington are two significant models for revitalizing senior faculty. They share certain commonalities: (1) each in its own way provides *a new collegial social structure* that facilitates dialogue about teaching and learning; (2) in both cases, the approach fosters a kind of *authentic dialogue* and the acquisition of new skills and insights in an endogenous fashion; (3) both efforts are *classroom-focused, student-centered;* and (4) both provide a timely response to the felt needs of senior faculty for *more leadership opportunities and challenge in their work.* Both approaches see teaching, learning, and community building as related, complex, long-term issues. Both presume that change will be a slow and gradual, developmental process.

On opposite coasts of the United States, two states—New Jersey and Washington—made relatively modest investments in statewide faculty development centers. The roots, focus, and operating styles of the New Jersey Center and the Washington Center differ substantially and both are clearly evolving organizations. Nonetheless, each of these centers clearly provides the respective state's higher education institutions with an important resource. It is not coincidental that some of the leading statewide work in cultural pluralism, calculus reform, women's studies, writing and thinking across the curriculum, and assessment is taking place in Washington and New Jersey. And leaders in the education community in both states believe they have barely scratched the surface of what can be accomplished. Once a sizable cadre of committed faculty and administrators become empowered to change the educational system, a powerful momentum for continuing reform is created. The New Jersey and Washington centers provide good examples of what states can do to support faculty development.

It is significant that both the New Jersey and Washington centers are ongoing, evolving organizations, and that they work across institutions. We believe third-party organizations like these two centers can play a unique role in improving higher education. While the state role in postsecondary education is seldom conceived in this fashion, we think states can benefit substantially by making relatively modest investments in ongoing interinstitutional

support systems like the New Jersey and Washington centers. By locating, organizing, and leveraging the talent scattered throughout a higher education system, statewide centers can become energy amplification systems. By providing structures and opportunities for bringing people together, they can open up a productive dialogue about undergraduate education, and help faculty and administrators create a new sense of common enterprise.

References

Austin, A., and Baldwin, R. *Faculty Collaboration.* ASHE-ERIC Higher Education Research Report, no. 7. Washington, D.C.: ASHE-ERIC Higher Education Reports, George Washington University, 1992.

Gabelnick, F., MacGregor, J., Matthews, R., and Smith, B. L. *Learning Communities: Creating Connections Among Students, Faculty, and Disciplines.* New Directions for Teaching and Learning, no. 41. San Francisco: Jossey-Bass, 1990.

Gabelnick, F., Matthews, R., MacGregor, J., and Smith, B. L. "Learning Communities and General Education." *Perspectives,* 1992, *22,* 104–121.

Golin, S. "Four Arguments for Peer Collaboration and Student Interviewing: The Master Faculty Program." *AAHE Bulletin: Teaching and Learning,* 1990, *43* (4), 9–10.

Goodsell, A., Maher, M., Tinto, V., Smith, B. L., and MacGregor, J. *Collaborative Learning: A Sourcebook for Higher Education.* University Park, Pa.: National Center on Postsecondary Teaching, Learning, and Assessment, 1992.

Graff, G. "How to Deal with the Humanities Crisis: Organize It." *ADE Bulletin,* 1990, no. 95, 4–10.

Katz, J. "Learning to Help Students Learn." *Liberal Education,* 1987, *73* (1), 28.

Katz, J., and Henry, M. *Turning Professors into Teachers.* New York: ACE/Macmillan, 1988.

Morrissey, P. (ed.). *Essays by Coordinators and Participants in the New Jersey Master Faculty Program.* Princeton, N.J.: Woodrow Wilson National Fellowship Fund, 1990.

New Jersey Institute for Collegiate Teaching and Learning. *Partners in Learning Handbook.* New Jersey Institute for Collegiate Teaching and Learning, 1991.

Palmer, P. "Divided No More: A Movement Approach to Educational Reform." *Change,* 1992, *24* (2), 10–17.

Rice, R. E., and Cheldelin, S. I. *The Knower and the Known: Making the Connection: Evaluation of the New Jersey Master Faculty Program.* Princeton, N.J.: Woodrow Wilson National Fellowship Foundation, 1989.

Smith, B. L. "The Washington Center: A Grassroots Approach to Faculty Development and Curricular Reform." *To Improve the Academy,* 1988, 8.

Smith, B. L. "Taking Structure Seriously." *Liberal Education,* 1991, *77,* 42–48.

Smith, B. L. "Team Teaching and Interdisciplinary Studies." In K. Prichard and R. M. Sawyer (eds.), *Handbook of College Teaching: Theory and Applications.* Westport, Conn.: Greenwood, forthcoming.

Smith, B. L., and Hunter, R. "Learning Communities: A Paradigm for Educational Revitalization." *Community College Review,* 1988, *15* (4), 45–51.

Smith, M. J., Golin, S., and Friedman, E. "Cosmopolitan Communities for Faculty Developers." *To Improve the Academy,* 1992, 7, 167–174.

Smith, M. J., and LaCelle-Peterson, M. "The Professor as Active Learner: Lessons from the New Jersey Master Faculty Program." *To Improve the Academy,* 1991, *10,* 271–278.

Tussman, J. *Experiment at Berkeley.* London: Oxford University Press, 1969.

BARBARA LEIGH SMITH is academic dean at *The Evergreen State College, Washington. She is also director of the Washington Center for Improving the Quality of Undergraduate Education.*

MYRNA J. SMITH is professor and faculty development chair at *Raritan Valley Community College, New Jersey. She currently serves as faculty fellow, New Jersey Institute for Collegiate Teaching and Learning.*

Senior faculty constitute a plentiful and largely untapped resource at a time when resources for higher education are exceedingly scarce and overtaxed.

The Senior Faculty: Higher Education's Plentiful Yet Largely Untapped Resource

Martin J. Finkelstein, Nina Dorset Jemmott

Village elders, having attained status and stature in their villages by virtue of their longevity, experience, and wisdom, played central roles in upholding traditions, socializing the young, and maintaining the culture of the village. But villages eventually grew into towns and then into cities, and the role and function of the village elder seemed no longer to be useful or valued. The elders became disenchanted with society because they were disregarded and unrewarded. In a quandry about what to do with their wise but troublesome elders, the villagers cum townspeople and city folk turned to other more pressing problems. The elders withdrew into themselves, accepted their lot, and waited for retirement.

American higher education no longer has the luxury of neglecting our most seasoned academics, the senior faculty, metaphorically our village elders—nor should we! All of the available evidence assembled in this volume suggests that the vast majority of midcareer and senior faculty are interested in teaching and in working with students—more interested, perhaps, than at any other time in their careers. And chances are they are as productive and vital in this and other areas as they were earlier in their careers.

Some senior faculty do not, however, fit the majority profile. Variously estimated to number between 10 and 33 percent of the professoriate, these individuals have by their isolation, oppositionalism, and disengagement from their colleagues and departments effectively detracted from the performance of the enterprise and challenged administrative patience and skill. While we have, as yet, little information on the impact of faculty disillusionment and disengagement on student learning, we do know that values and

New DIRECTIONS FOR TEACHING AND LEARNING, no. 55, Fall 1993 © Jossey-Bass Publishers

attitudes are communicated through how and what we do, that is, by how and what we teach. The literature shows that senior faculty are consistent in their love of teaching and of their students, in spite of varying organizational climates and individual career difficulties.

But if the central message of this volume were to be encapsulated in a single sentence, that sentence might read: *senior faculty constitute a plentiful and largely untapped resource at a time when resources for higher education are exceedingly scarce and overtaxed.* A provocative message indeed!

The authors' various experiences and studies offer definitions of senior faculty and explanations for the plight of senior faculty that account for our use of the analogy linking senior faculty with village elders. Some chapters offer suggestions for revitalization of senior faculty in their teaching and research roles, and others describe institutional and statewide models found useful in beginning and sustaining conversations about senior faculty.

Successful efforts to revitalize and sustain senior faculty had critical elements in common. Prominent among them is an extraordinary amount of collaboration between faculty. Obviously, teamwork is required to build strong programs and to establish lasting coalitions. Another common element is the amount of time involved, anywhere from one to ten years, not only to develop new institutional configurations and relationships but also to institutionalize a view of senior faculty that sees them as important and valued assets of the institution. In essence, in tapping the resources of senior faculty, there are no "quick fixes" for either organizational or individual arenas.

Reward structures were also a prominent feature of revitalization efforts. Reward in intrinsic and extrinsic forms was viewed by senior faculty themselves as energizing and motivating. Overtures as simple as praise and recognition were almost as important as merit pay or other tangible sources of appreciation and expressions of care about the senior faculty and their work.

While professional vitality in one's teaching, and indeed in one's career more generally, is doubtlessly in part a function of individual differences (vital people are born that way), it is nonetheless also clearly affected by organizational climate and administrative intervention. Boice described two successful strategies for reengaging "middle-aged disillusioned" faculty: mentoring programs and growth contracting (cataloguing). LaCelle-Peterson and Finkelstein reported the success of interventions aimed at restructuring the faculty member's teaching situation (team teaching; course clustering; common examinations in multisection courses), and at providing opportunities for individual professional growth.

Three common threads run through these reports. First, the central place of collegiality—that is, vitality in teaching, no less than in research—is promoted and sustained by interaction with like-minded colleagues, be it one-on-one or in a group situation. Second, there is a critical need to break up

routines, to change either the nature of work responsibilities or the work set-ting, or, periodically, both. Third, there is a need for organizational and ad-ministrative intervention. Evidence shows that the opportunities that faculty take advantage of tend to be organizationally created either by (a) direct ad-ministrative initiative (mentoring programs; chairs preparing for their role as human resource managers); (b) brokering or otherwise mediating external opportunities (for example, through fellowships and exchanges); or (c) es-tablishing vehicles such as growth contracting, for structuring faculty self-reflection and self-steering.

We find concrete illustrations of these common threads throughout the volume. Braid's, Farmer's, and Smith and Smith's chapters chronicle the de-sign and support of faculty networks focused on curricular revision and/or specific classroom issues. Curriculum is, of course, the time-honored win-dow on faculty members' disciplinary and instructional commitments. Smith and Smith, in particular, remind us of the always important extrainstitutional dimension to faculty collegiality—what Rice has called the *cosmopolitan* di-mension of the teaching role.

Both Boice's and Farmer's chapters report the successful development of vehicles such as growth contracting for self-assessment and the collaborative identification of professional development opportunities, and the value of pressing colleagues and administrators into service as confederates in faculty professional development.

Finally, both Boice's and Jackson and Simpson's chapters illustrate mod-els for mentoring programs that, in effect, establish "new" networks for "old" faculty by pairing them with their junior colleagues.

The concept of intergenerational mentoring (faculty generations, that is) is one of enormous import as higher education prepares for the entry of an increasing cohort of new faculty. The emerging pattern at many institutions suggests the potential risk that our seasoned faculty, who are responsible in large part for socializing new and junior faculty, may find themselves "pitted against" their junior colleagues along at least two dimensions.

First, there is the matter of the changing rewards system at historically teaching-oriented institutions. Many nonresearch universities are hiring new, research-oriented faculty from our best graduate schools and emphasiz-ing research and publication in their promotion and tenure decisions, in ef-fect "dispossessing" many senior faculty who were hired and socialized under a decidedly teaching-oriented regime. Senior faculty—the village elders of our metaphor—find themselves out of place and out of step with the new and emerging traditions of the workplace.

Second, there is the related matter of salary compression: in many fields, market forces are driving up the entry-level salaries of new hires—sometimes above the salaries of their senior colleagues. Both Boice's and Jackson and Simpson's work suggest that senior faculty can find in their junior colleagues

a source of validation and a vehicle for constructive self-reflection on their own teaching and careers and ultimately for reengagement with their departments and their campuses.

Taken together, this collection has, we believe, set out a challenging agenda for academic administrators (from department chairs on up) to create supportive organizational structures and for senior faculty themselves to devise strategies for their own revitalization. As Robert Boice reminds us, we have chosen to assume that *our seasoned faculty have gotten the careers they deserve.* If we have learned anything from the work represented here, it is, *that is not true!*

American higher education ought not to allow senior faculty to go the way of the village elder, but must find ways—and we are doing just that—to utilize our most abundant and heretofore largely untapped resource. If we accept the challenge, the 1990s will come to be known as the decade of the senior faculty—perhaps the most promising decade in our history.

MARTIN J. FINKELSTEIN is director of the New Jersey Institute for Collegiate Teaching and Learning at Seton Hall University, South Orange, New Jersey.

NINA DORSET JEMMOTT is associate director of the New Jersey Institute for Collegiate Teaching and Learning at Seton Hall University, South Orange, New Jersey.

These resources serve as a guide for administrators, faculty developers, and faculty themselves who seek to design effective institutional interventions that enhance the work and careers of senior faculty.

Resources for Developing Senior Faculty as Teachers

Robert K. Seal

This volume presents a wide range of perspectives on the roles of senior faculty in higher education. While there are differences in the issues senior faculty face, strikingly common themes emerge that command special attention by the higher education community, particularly, the predictable midlife career crisis, the importance of collegial networks and mentoring, and the responsibility of institutions for "brokering" development opportunities. The resources contained in this appendix illuminate these common themes by focusing our sights on the current needs of senior faculty and potentially effective institutional interventions. Designed as a "quick reference" resource for administrators, faculty developers, and faculty leaders, this is by no means an exhaustive inventory. Rather, the sources listed here have been selected to illustrate the breadth of information in areas of particular relevance to senior faculty.

The resources have been divided into four major categories: research on senior faculty, personnel policies for senior faculty, strategies and programs for revitalizing and engaging senior faculty, and tools for self-assessment of campus teaching climates. Each category provides a summary of pertinent literature generated over the last ten years.

The sources listed under Research on Senior Faculty offer a profile of senior faculty, exploring the place of teaching among their many roles as teachers, researchers, and scholars. Topics range from a broad, comprehensive

The author wishes to acknowledge the assistance of Marya Burke, a 1992–1993 intern at the New Jersey Institute for Collegiate Teaching and Learning, in compiling these resources.

review of the state of the professoriate, to more practical aspects of career options and career development opportunities.

Personnel Policies for Senior Faculty includes both profession-wide and institution-specific procedures that attempt to assess senior faculty work, specifically, tenure review and posttenure evaluation. Information on growth contracting is included as one vehicle for fostering faculty development.

Strategies and Programs for Vitalizing and Engaging Senior Faculty illustrate successful programs designed to benefit senior faculty. Statewide programs, such as Partners in Learning in New Jersey, as well as federally funded grant initiatives, such as the Senior Mentoring Service at Temple University, are illustrated. The role of the administrator in supporting the development of senior faculty is also examined.

The final resource category, Self-Assessment of Campus Teaching Climates, offers three practical audits that institutions can use to assess the level of support for senior faculty development on their campus. The audits examine the traditional roles of teaching, research, and service, as well as other institutional issues such as leadership, organizational climate, and academic practices.

Research on Senior Faculty

These resources reflect a broad range of literature on senior faculty, particularly with respect to their roles as teachers, researchers, and scholars. Of particular interest is faculty career development.

Armour, R. "Senior Faculty Careers and Personal Development: A Survey." Paper presented at the annual meeting of the American Educational Research Association, San Francisco, Mar. 1989.

Over 1,100 senior faculty in Virginia were surveyed regarding job satisfaction, and community, personal, and career matters. Findings suggest that "aging faculty remain internally controlled, vital, and productive"; job satisfaction is high, and does not vary by race, gender, or academic discipline. Overall, this survey reports generally good faculty morale, a high level of job satisfaction, and continued vitality.

Baldwin, R. G. Expanding Faculty Options: Career Development Projects at Colleges and Universities. Washington, D.C.: American Association for Higher Education, 1981.

Campus-based programs that seek to retool faculty for alternative careers are described in this document. Spanning career planning, respecialization and retraining, experiential projects, multidimensional career services, and academic transition projects, this report cites twenty-five individual programs across the country that address the special needs of senior faculty. Each entry gives a brief description of the program, information

regarding costs and outcomes, and other available material, including a contact person for further information.

Baldwin, R. G., and Blackburn, R. T. (eds.). *College Faculty: Versatile Human Resources in a Period of Constraint.* New Directions for Institutional Research, no. 40. San Francisco: Jossey-Bass, 1983.

Is higher education realistic in its expectations of its faculty? Perhaps not. Baldwin and Blackburn suggest the need for a reexamination of the basic premises of faculty employment policies in light of concurrent calls for maintaining institutional vitality through faculty development. The authors point to the career paths of professionals in other organizations as a means of comparison for college faculty.

Bowen, H. R., and Schuster, J. H. *American Professors: A National Resource Imperiled.* New York: Oxford University Press, 1986.

The complexion of the American professoriate has undergone a significant transformation in recent years, as higher education reacts to changes in enrollment, demographics, and financial support. Bowen and Schuster base their findings on data collected from over five hundred faculty interviews nationally. They characterize the professoriate's background, abilities, values, and productivity. Included is a profile of the state of the profession: rewards and working conditions, the academic labor market, and the prospects for future employment opportunities. The authors consider the potential turnover within academe in the next two decades, and offer suggestions for recruiting or retraining faculty to fill the teaching roles.

Clark, B. *The Academic Life: Small Worlds, Different Worlds.* Princeton, N.J.: Carnegie Foundation for the Advancement of Teaching, 1987.

Clark's study of academic life, based on data collected from five thousand faculty members in the 1984 Carnegie Foundation Faculty Survey, looks at the culture and characteristics of the profession: its foundations, the dimensions of academic professionalism, and the logic of the profession. Focusing on the functions of teaching and research, Clark interweaves the diversity within academic life with the structures that act as controlling and defining agents (for example, disciplines). The author concentrates on the many aspects of the academic "culture" that exist in higher education today.

Crawley, A. L. "Meeting the Challenge of an Aging Professoriate: An Opportunity for Leadership." *To Improve the Academy,* 1990, 9, 231–243. Also, *National Survey on Senior Faculty Renewal.* Athens: University of Georgia Press, 1993.

Crawley provides a critique of recent research on faculty productivity and aging. He reviews the implications of uncapping the mandatory retirement age, the myths associated with an "aging" faculty, and the resulting

challenge for university leaders to provide a structure for senior faculty renewal. This literature review is the context for a survey in progress of faculty and academic administrators at 104 research universities across the country on issues that directly affect senior faculty careers and retirement options. The results, to be made available in July 1993, will provide a detailed picture of faculty development–related programs and personnel policies that affect senior faculty.

El-Khawas, E. *Senior Faculty in Academe: Active, Committed to the Teaching Role.* Research Briefs, vol. 2, no. 5. Washington, D.C.: American Council on Education, 1991.

This report provides an empirical profile of senior faculty, gleaned from three recent national surveys: Higher Education Research Institute (1989), Carnegie Foundation (1989), and American Council on Education (1972–73). The report gives particular emphasis to teaching activities and attitudes regarding teaching. Senior faculty are explored in terms of several lines: demographics, career milestones, regular professional activities, attitudes, and future career plans. "This profile suggests that most senior faculty are productive, contributing members of the academic professions, who are particularly active in teaching of undergraduates, an endeavor that senior faculty value."

Finkelstein, M. J. *The American Academic Profession.* Columbus: Ohio State University Press, 1984.

This book presents an in-depth look at full-time faculty through the lens of social scientific inquiry. The professorial role is traced from the latter half of the eighteenth century through World War II, with specific emphasis on the growth of the academic profession since World War II. Contemporary research is synthesized under three basic categories: career paths, how faculty go about their work, and life outside their work roles. Finkelstein discusses the history of the academic role, and addresses the case of women and minority faculty.

Rice, R. E. "Dreams and Actualities: Danforth Fellows in Mid-Career." *American Association for Higher Education Bulletin,* 1980, 32, 3–5, 14–16.

To explore the needs of college and university faculty in midcareer, the Danforth Foundation in 1975 invited three hundred fellows to two faculty workshops on the profession of teaching. The fellows represented three distinct academic generations: those who began their academic careers in the 1950s, those who completed their doctorates in the mid-1960s, and those who received graduate fellowships for women in the years 1965 to 1970. The fellows were asked to respond to statements regarding personal and professional aspirations they themselves had written when first applying for the fel-

lowships. Responses varied across the three generations, reflecting the changes in social conditions and the changes in the direction of higher education over the twenty-year period. The fellows discussed topics ranging from the impact of teaching religious and ethical values, to career satisfaction, to the struggles of female faculty in achieving their career goals.

Personnel Policies for Senior Faculty

These resources review personnel policies and procedures related to faculty evaluation, principally the issue of tenure and posttenure review. Included are policy statements from national organizations on academic freedom as well as studies that assess the various forms of posttenure evaluation.

Review of Tenured Faculty

American Association of University Professors. *Academic Freedom and Tenure, 1940 Statement of Principles and 1970 Interpretive Comments*. AAUP Policy Documents and Reports. Washington, D.C.: American Association of University Professors, 1977.

    This is the official document issued by the American Association of University Professors supporting academic freedom and tenure on college campuses. Constructed for publication in 1940, it has remained fundamentally unchanged in fifty years.

American Association of University Professors. "On Periodic Evaluation of Tenured Faculty: A Discussion at Wingspread, Aug. 24–26, 1983." *Academe*, 1983, *69* (6), 1a, 14a.

    A joint conference sponsored by the American Council on Education (ACE) and the American Association of University Professors (AAUP) convened to address the issue of posttenure evaluation. This statement was issued, reaffirming a commitment to the existing principles of academic freedom and tenure. This statement reflects the consensus of the conference participants; it is not a policy statement by ACE or AAUP.

Andrews, H. A., and Licata, C. M. "Administrative Perceptions of Existing Evaluation Systems." *Journal of Personnel Evaluation in Education*, 1991, *5* (1), 69–76.

    Administrators from two-year colleges were surveyed about their perceptions of the merits of faculty review and the existing faculty evaluation programs on their campuses. Of the 199 deans and vice presidents surveyed, 70 percent reported that some form of posttenure evaluation existed at their institution; however, the responses did not support a strong positive or negative sentiment about existing faculty evaluation procedures and policies.

Chait, R., and Ford, A. *Beyond Traditional Tenure*. San Francisco: Jossey-Bass, 1982.

In this "Guide to Sound Policies and Practice," Chait and Ford discuss the various structural forms that tenure has taken and the problems and benefits of each form. Data for this work were obtained from many different sources, including visits to national associations (such as the American Association of University Professors, the American Council on Education, and the Association of Governing Boards), as well as from questionnaires sent to seven hundred senior administrators throughout the country. The authors suggest some alternatives to traditional tenure practices, using case studies as illustrations, including extended probationary periods, term contracts, and changes in tenure quotas. Chait and Ford include information on evaluating tenured faculty, distributing rewards and applying sanctions, and auditing and improving faculty personnel systems.

Licata, C. M. "An Investigation of the Status of Post-Tenure Faculty Evaluation in Selected Community Colleges." Paper presented at the ninth annual meeting of the Association for the Study of Higher Education, Chicago, Mar. 1985.

In a survey of 857 faculty and administrators from nine community colleges, 77 percent of those surveyed indicated that their institution employed some form of posttenure evaluation. Faculty development was considered a primary rationale for such evaluation plans. Fifty-nine percent of the administrators and 49.6 percent of the faculty reported that the primary purpose of pretenure evaluation was to provide information relating to personnel decisions. These pre- and posttenure evaluation plans raised questions by the respondents, as over 88 percent felt that some other form of evaluation plan or criteria was warranted in order to better assess the strengths and weaknesses of individual faculty.

Licata, C. M. *Post-Tenure Faculty Evaluation*. Washington, D.C.: ASHE-ERIC Clearinghouse on Higher Education, 1987.

Is posttenure evaluation a threat to academic tenure? Not according to the proponents of posttenure evaluation, who suggest that it is a formative means "to reinforce faculty growth and improve instruction," as long as it is not used as grounds for dismissal, and that if dismissal is warranted, academic due process must be strictly followed. Opponents fear that it will devalue pretenure evaluation and may erode camaraderie on campus. For the institution considering posttenure evaluation, Licata offers practical steps for preimplementation attention.

Reisman, B. "Performance Evaluation for Tenured Faculty: Issues and Research." *Liberal Education*, 1986, 72 (1), 73–87.

Reisman discusses the results of a survey of 104 faculty and administrators at twenty-six universities regarding the use of performance evaluation of

tenured and nontenured faculty. Although many strong opinions exist about the relative merits of performance evaluations, there seems to be no consensus across the profession. In fact, there seems to be confusion within institutions as to the purpose, standards, and uses of posttenure evaluation. A prevailing pattern of decentralized, informal, and unsystematic performance reviews is common. Despite this lack of structure, receptivity to performance evaluations of faculty is higher than expected.

Wesson, M., and Johnson, S. "Post-Tenure Review and Faculty Revitalization." *Academe,* 1991, 77 (3), 53–57.

The posttenure peer review program at the University of Colorado was scrutinized by the researchers, with the goal of making recommendations about the continuation of the program to the board of regents. Faculty, department chairs, and deans who had been involved in peer review in the last ten years were surveyed. Several trends emerged: (1) posttenure review was promising, but had little impact on faculty revitalization; (2) too much time and energy was required; (3) unproductive faculty were "known" quantities; (4) the definition of what constitutes a "good" and "productive" faculty member was constantly changing. The weakness of this program was the lack of resources to effect a change once a faculty member's developmental needs had been identified.

Growth Contracting

Furniss, W. "Reshaping Faculty Careers." *Change,* 1981, 13 (7), 38–45, 57.

Furniss profiles seven faculty members to illustrate problems that academics may face at different stages in their careers. These profiles suggest that faculty may not be prepared for the realities of academic life, and that their professional lives are considerably different from their expectations. The implications for faculty development through growth contracting and career planning are elucidated, as faculty search to modify their academic careers.

Geller, W. "Professional Growth Contracting." *Journal of the NAWDAC,* 1982, 45 (2), 20–21.

Geller discusses the merits and uses of professional growth contracting with specific attention to encouraging staff to identify their individual needs for development. The author describes one such program as a model, used by a student affairs staff for growth contracting within their department.

Simpson, E., and Oggel, T. *Growth Contracting for Faculty Development.* Manhattan, Kans.: Center for Faculty Evaluation and Development in Higher Education, 1984.

The authors define the applications and limitations of growth contracts, as well as critical steps in the successful development of the plans. This bind-

ing agreement delineates specific goals to be accomplished by the faculty member entering into the contract. Several imperatives for the program are listed, including a healthy collegial relationship between the faculty and contract coordinator, and consistent monitoring of the plan once the contract has gone into effect. Contracting is suggested as a useful tool in curriculum and program development, as well as for the acquisition of new research skills and experiences.

Strategies and Programs for Vitalizing and Engaging Senior Faculty

These resources illustrate some of the programmatic approaches that have been designed to facilitate senior faculty's reinvestment in their careers. Beginning with mentoring and team teaching, they also review general strategies for engaging senior faculty, highlighting roles of the department chair and other academic administrators in revitalizing classroom teaching.

Mentoring Programs

Boice, R. "Mentoring New Faculty: A Program for Implementation." *Journal of Staff, Program, and Organization Development,* 1990, 8 (3), 143–160.
    Boice describes a two-year study of twenty-five pairs of mentors and protégés at a comprehensive university that coupled senior faculty with their younger colleagues in both within-discipline and across-discipline dyads. The process of mentoring is examined along several dimensions, including a comparison of traditional (within-discipline) and nontraditional (across-discipline) mentoring, an examination of what mentors and protégés do/do not do spontaneously and efficiently, and a description of a practical program for mentoring that includes periodic evaluations from mentoring pairs and external observers. The strength of this research is its empirical evaluation of the process of mentoring.

Boice, R. "Lessons Learned About Mentoring." In M. D. Sorcinelli and A. E. Austin (eds.), *Developing New and Junior Faculty.* New Directions for Teaching and Learning, no. 50. San Francisco: Jossey-Bass, 1992.
    Boice reviews the current literature on mentoring and discusses two main issues: the shortcomings that have evolved out of current mentoring practices, and the practical guidelines for optimizing mentoring programs. The author suggests that even the most flourishing mentoring programs may be too passive in their structure, thus hindering the opportunity for interventions. Boice goes on to describe traditional and nontraditional mentoring styles, and the elements, benefits, and problems of each.

Fund for the Improvement of Postsecondary Education. *The Senior Mentoring Service: Sustaining and Strengthening a Teaching Culture.* Washington, D.C.: Fund for the Improvement of Postsecondary Education, 1991.

This document provides a detailed description of a mentoring program at Temple University that matches retired faculty with new or junior faculty members. The pairs work together on pedagogy, career development, and the politics of working in a large institution. This project is unique in that the mentors come exclusively from the ranks of retired faculty, which limits the judgmental aspects that could arise in mentoring situations. The pairs submit periodic reports to the project director, and the interaction is left up to the individuals involved. There are also workshops and summer grants to supplement the program.

Fund for the Improvement of Postsecondary Education. *Preparing Future Faculty.* Washington, D.C.: Fund for the Improvement of Postsecondary Education, 1992.

To aid in the preparation of college teachers through interventions offered during graduate school, the Council of Independent Colleges has developed a program that couples graduate students from research universities with senior faculty mentors at liberal arts colleges, to help develop a better understanding of faculty roles in undergraduate colleges. Graduate students in this program taught courses, attended teaching skills seminars, and advised undergraduates as part of their preparation experience.

Merrian, S. B. "Mentoring in Higher Education: What We Know Now." *Review of Higher Education,* 1987, *11* (2), 199–210.

Twenty-six studies on mentoring were reviewed, including faculty-to-faculty, faculty-to-student, and administrator-to-administrator pairs. This research revealed that little formal study has been done on faculty-to-faculty and faculty-to-student mentoring, and raised two basic questions: How can conclusions about the effectiveness of mentoring be drawn? Are changes realistic reflections of the mentoring process?

Murray, R. C. *The TACT-Mentor Program: A Dual Introduction into College Teaching Final Report.* Washington, D.C.: Fund for the Improvement of Postsecondary Education, 1989.

TACT (Teachers and College Teaching) was funded by the Fund for the Improvement of Postsecondary Education (FIPSE) as a one-year mentoring project for college teachers at Heidelberg College, Ohio. Divided into two parts, the initial component involved a discussion by new faculty of Joseph Lowman's book, *Mastering the Techniques of Teaching.* Murray found that as a result of their interactions over a ten-week period, fourteen new faculty from highly diverse backgrounds achieved a sense of community within the

group, as well as a heightened use of innovative teaching methods and a greater sense of belonging to the academic community. The second phase coupled senior faculty with new faculty in across-discipline dyads for a completely unstructured mentoring program. Discussion of the successes and failures of this loosely coupled program are included by the author.

Sands, R. G., Parson, L. A., and Duane, J. "Faculty Mentoring Faculty in a Public University." *Journal of Higher Education,* 1991, *62* (2), 174–193.
      This study of 347 faculty at a public midwestern university addressed the issue of the complexity and multiplicity of mentoring situations in American higher education. Over 72 percent of the faculty interviewed stated that they had had a mentor sometime during their educational career, most frequently during graduate school. Only one-third of the respondents reported having a mentor during their beginning faculty years. Mentors who were described as friend, career guide, information source, and intellectual guide were considered the most beneficial to their mentees.

Team Teaching

Austin, A. E., and Baldwin, R. G. *Faculty Collaboration: Enhancing the Quality of Scholarship and Teaching.* ASHE-ERIC Higher Education Reports, no. 7. Washington, D.C.: Association for the Study of Higher Education, 1991.
      Research on the dramatic growth of, and interest in, faculty collaboration is examined by the authors. Explored is the rationale for faculty collaboration, key steps in establishing a collaborative venture, controversy that surrounds joint efforts in teaching and research, and recommendations for fostering collaboration for faculty, administrators, and the higher education community. The authors discuss the practical aspects of establishing a collaborative effort between faculty, and its implications for faculty development.

MacGregor, J. "Collaborative Learning: Shared Inquiry as a Process of Reform." In M. D. Svinicki (ed.), *The Changing Face of College Teaching.* New Directions for Teaching and Learning, no. 42. San Francisco: Jossey-Bass, 1990.
      MacGregor traces the historical construct of collaborative learning, beginning with its inception in education. She discusses theoretical aspects of collaborative learning, and indicates the need for changes in attitudes and role definition of both student and teacher in order for this type of learning to be effectively implemented.

Strategies for Engaging Senior Faculty

Baldwin, R. G. *Incentives for Faculty Vitality.* New Directions for Higher Education, no. 51. San Francisco: Jossey-Bass, 1985.

Two important questions about senior faculty are raised in this book: What keeps a faculty member vital? What incentives can an institution offer to foster vitality? Baldwin examines the public's perceptions of dissatisfaction with faculty, and uses that dissatisfaction as a point of departure for determining ways to enhance faculty vitality. Baldwin assesses what the incentives are, who should develop them, and what incentives should be most effective. Incentives for faculty revitalization are illustrated from both the collegiate and corporate perspectives.

Boice, R. "Faculty Development via Field Programs for Middle-Aged, Disillusioned Faculty." *Research in Higher Education,* 1986, 25 (2), 115–135.

Boice offers ways of reengaging disengaged middle-aged faculty in this report. Field-based faculty developers, including department chairs, are schooled in a systematic format for reestablishing communication and reinvolvement by "problem" faculty. Included is a profile of the middle-aged, disillusioned faculty, problems associated with reengaging colleagues, and the benefits for field-based developers.

Clark, S., and Lewis, D. *Faculty Vitality and Institutional Productivity: Critical Perspectives for Higher Education.* New York: Teachers College Press, 1985.

Clark and Lewis have compiled a sourcebook on faculty vitality and institutional productivity that includes institutional policy options and demographic and external pressures. The sourcebook features articles on career development, aging and productivity, and individual and organizational contributions to faculty vitality. Maintaining faculty vitality is considered via faculty development, midcareer change options, outside professional consulting, collective bargaining, and early retirement options.

Lucas, A. F. (ed.). *The Department Chairperson's Role in Enhancing College Teaching.* New Directions for Teaching and Learning, no. 37. San Francisco: Jossey-Bass, 1989.

The quality of undergraduate education and who bears the responsibility for ensuring its high standards is the focus of this book. The various contributors argue that this responsibility of "creating a learning climate" should be held by department chairs and the academic department as a unit. The authors offer advice to department chairs on how to suggest changes and implement plans, including creative uses of classroom technologies, ways to actively involve the students in learning, and training programs for teaching assistants.

Seldin, P., and Associates. *How Administrators Can Improve Teaching: Moving from Talk to Action in Higher Education.* San Francisco: Jossey-Bass, 1990.

The book consists of eleven individual papers on specific methods for improving teaching, from assessing the university climate and its effect on teaching, to the importance of campus and department leadership and the

appropriate use of evaluative information, to practical, real-world examples and suggestions for improving teaching and learning. It contains literature reviews and personal anecdotes, experiences, and analyses.

Smith, B. L. "Taking Structure Seriously: The Learning Community Model." *Liberal Education*, 1991, 77 (2), 42–48.

The learning community model has evolved as an alternative to traditional methods of teaching and learning, for it links courses, faculty, and students together in an environment that fosters intellectual interaction and active learning. Learning communities' pedagogy may include team teaching, interdisciplinary content, integration of skill and content teaching, and active approaches to learning. As a faculty development tool, learning communities have rekindled "the creative side of teaching and provide new challenges" for senior faculty, because faculty involved in learning communities literally re-create the curriculum, establishing a "climate of growth, trust, permission, and personal responsibility—key elements in self-renewal."

Smith, M. J., and LaCelle-Peterson, M. W. "The Professor as Active Learner: Lessons from the New Jersey Master Faculty Program." *To Improve the Academy*, 1991, *10*, 271–278.

Smith and LaCelle-Peterson describe the New Jersey Master Faculty Program (now Partners in Learning [PIL]), which brings together pairs of faculty to talk about teaching and learning in a nonevaluative and nonjudgmental environment. Each faculty member observes the other's class, interviews students, and meets with other faculty participants to discuss their experiences. Together, the partners share a common teaching experience and examine the connections between faculty teaching and student learning.

Self-Assessment of Campus Teaching Climates

These resources offer self-assessment techniques, including audits that have been designed for colleges interested in supporting faculty through discussion and analysis of the campus climate. These audits aid institutional assessment of policies and practices that impinge on classroom teaching from several different perspectives.

Austin, A. E., Rice, R. E., and Splete, A. P. *The Academic Workplace Audit.* Washington, D.C.: Council of Independent Colleges, 1991.

The audit is a tool for institutions interested in "supporting faculty morale and the quality of the academic workplace." Developed by the Council of Independent Colleges for use by small colleges, it can be adapted to inspire discussion of similar issues at larger universities. The audit is divided into Primary Factors (organizational culture, leadership, organizational promise and momentum, and institutional identification coupled with institutional

diversity), and Related Factors (support for scholarship, faculty development, balance of intrinsic and extrinsic rewards, the nature of colleagueship, and college-community relations).

Chickering, A. W., Gamson, Z. F., and Barsi, L. M. *Seven Principles for Good Practice in Undergraduate Education: Faculty Inventory.* Also *Institutional Inventory.* Racine, Wash.: Johnson Foundation, 1989.

Under the auspices of the American Association for Higher Education, the Education Commission of the States, and the Johnson Foundation, these inventories were designed to help faculty members, departments, colleges, and universities examine individual behaviors and institutional policies and practices for their consistency with "Seven Principles for Good Practice in Undergraduate Education." Each inventory is divided into six sections: climate, academic practices, curriculum, faculty, academic and student support services, and facilities. Best when used as a diagnostic instrument, the inventories can be used to improve teaching and "create more educationally powerful environments."

Lovett, C. M. "Vitality Without Mobility: The Faculty Opportunities Audit." *Current Issues in Higher Education,* no. 4. Washington, D.C.: American Association for Higher Education, 1983–84.

The potential for career development and professional growth is evaluated with this audit of faculty opportunities. The audit focuses on the traditional activities of teaching, research, and service, as well as professional growth through the expansion of traditional roles, and the experiences of new professional roles. There are a series of questions for faculty, and a series for administrators, each designed to assess their institution's contribution to the professional growth of the faculty.

ROBERT K. SEAL *is research associate at the New Jersey Institute for Collegiate Teaching and Learning, Seton Hall University, South Orange, New Jersey.*

INDEX

Academic disciplines, changes in, 13
Administration, faculty coalition with, 57, 65-66
Admissions, with improved retention, 64
American Association for Higher Education (AAHE), National Assessment Forum, 44
American Association of University Professors, 103
Andrews, H. A., 103
Angelo, T., 46
Armour, R., 2, 100
Assessment. *See* Performance-based assessment; Self-assessment
Association of American Colleges (AAC), Cultural Legacies Project, 60, 61, 62
Astin, A. W., 8, 14
Austin, A., 30, 85, 108, 110

Baldwin, R. G., 2, 8, 12, 30, 37, 85, 100, 101, 108
Barsi, L. M., 110
Bayer, A. E., 8
Betz, R., 84
Bieber, J. P., 9, 12
Blackburn, R. T., 2, 8, 9, 12, 37, 101
Boice, R., 3, 9, 13, 14, 33, 38, 39, 41, 96, 97, 98, 106, 109
Bowen, H. R., 1, 8, 12, 101
Boyer, E., 17, 70
Braid, B., 3, 55, 58, 67, 97
Burke, D., 8, 12
Burke, M., 99n
Burn-out. *See* Disillusionment

Caffarella, R. S., 2
Caplow, T., 8
Career: of senior faculty, 12-13; turning points in, 37-38
Career ladder, 16
Carnegie Foundation for the Advancement of Teaching, 2, 8, 9, 14, 16
Cataloguing, as faculty development strategy, 39-40
Chait, R., 104
Cheldelin, S. I., 85
Chickering, A. W., 110

Clark, B., 8, 24, 37, 46, 101
Clark, S., 9, 109
Collaboration: opportunities for, 29-30; on teaching, 28
Colleagueship, lack of, 15, 26
Corcoran, M., 9
Crawley, A. L., 1, 101
Cross, K. P., 46
Curriculum, King's College reform of, 45-46

Danforth Fellows, study of, 10-11, 14-15
Departments: discussion of teaching in, 26-27; and faculty development, 30-31
Dey, E., 8, 14
Dialogue: among senior faculty, 92; shortage of, 15. *See also* Discussion
Diamond, R. M., 2
Disciplines. *See* Academic disciplines
Discussion: in Partners in Learning program, 84-85; of teaching, 26-27. *See also* Dialogue
Disillusionment: avoiding, 40-41; career turning points with, 37-38; faculty development strategies for, 38-40; problems exhibited by faculty with, 34-36; reasons for, 36-37
Dooris, M. S., 12
Driver, M. J., 17
Duane, J., 108

Edgerton, R., 2, 12
El-Khawas, E., 2, 102
Evaluation, of Senior Teaching Fellows program, 73-75
Evergreen State College, The, 87, 88
Exxon Foundation, 88

Faculty: career experiences for, 38; common problems with, 34-36; effect of Partners in Learning program on, 85-87; future demographics of, 1; Lilly Teaching Fellows program for junior, 71; pairing of, 83-84; shortage of, 1, 8. *See also* Faculty, midcareer; Faculty, senior

113

ORDERING INFORMATION

NEW DIRECTIONS FOR TEACHING AND LEARNING is a series of paperback books that presents ideas and techniques for improving college teaching, based both on the practical expertise of seasoned instructors and on the latest research findings of educational and psychological researchers. Books in the series are published quarterly in Spring, Summer, Fall, and Winter and are available for purchase by subscription and individually.

SUBSCRIPTIONS for 1993 cost $47.00 for individuals (a savings of 25 percent over single-copy prices) and $62.00 for institutions, agencies, and libraries. Please do not send institutional checks for personal subscriptions. Standing orders are accepted.

SINGLE COPIES cost $15.95 when payment accompanies order. (California, New Jersey, New York, and Washington, D.C., residents please include appropriate sales tax.) Billed orders will be charged postage and handling.

DISCOUNTS FOR QUANTITY ORDERS are available. Please write to the address below for information.

ALL ORDERS must include either the name of an individual or an official purchase order number. Please submit your order as follows:
    Subscriptions: specify series and year subscription is to begin
    Single copies: include individual title code (such as TL50)

MAIL ALL ORDERS TO:
    Jossey-Bass Publishers
    350 Sansome Street
    San Francisco, California 94104-1342

FOR SINGLE-COPY SALES OUTSIDE OF THE UNITED STATES CONTACT:
    Maxwell Macmillan International Publishing Group
    866 Third Avenue
    New York, New York 10022-6221

FOR SUBSCRIPTION SALES OUTSIDE OF THE UNITED STATES, contact any international subscription agency or Jossey-Bass directly.

**Statement of Ownership,
Management and
Circulation**
(Required by 39 U.S.C. 3685)

1A. Title of Publication	1B. PUBLICATION NO. (ISSN)	2. Date of Filing
NEW DIRECTIONS FOR TEACHING AND LEARNING	0 2 7 1 0 6 3 3	12/13/93

3. Frequency of Issue	3A. No. of Issues Published Annually	3B. Annual Subscription Price
Quarterly	Four (4)	$47.00(personal) $62.00(institutional)

4. Complete Mailing Address of Known Office of Publication *(Street, City, County, State and ZIP+4 Code) (Not printers)*

350 Sansome Street, San Francisco, CA 94104-1342 (San Francisco County)

5. Complete Mailing Address of the Headquarters of General Business Offices of the Publisher *(Not printer)*

(above address)

6. Full Names and Complete Mailing Address of Publisher, Editor, and Managing Editor *(This item MUST NOT be blank)*

Publisher *(Name and Complete Mailing Address)*

Jossey-Bass Inc., Publishers (above address)

Editor *(Name and Complete Mailing Address)*

Robert J. Menges, Center for the Teaching Professions, Northwestern Univ,
2003 Sheridan Road, Evanston, IL 60208-2610

Managing Editor *(Name and Complete Mailing Address)*

Lynn D. Luckow, President, Jossey-Bass Inc., Publishers (address above)

7. Owner *(If owned by a corporation, its name and address must be stated and also immediately thereunder the names and addresses of stockholders owning or holding 1 percent or more of total amount of stock. If not owned by a corporation, the names and addresses of the individual owners must be given. If owned by a partnership or other unincorporated firm, its name and address, as well as that of each individual must be given. If the publication is published by a nonprofit organization, its name and address must be stated.) (Item must be completed.)*

Full Name	Complete Mailing Address
Macmillan, Inc.	55 Railroad Avenue Greenwich, CT 06830-6378

8. Known Bondholders, Mortgagees, and Other Security Holders Owning or Holding 1 Percent or More of Total Amount of Bonds, Mortgages or Other Securities *(If there are none, so state)*

Full Name	Complete Mailing Address
same as above	same as above

9. For Completion by Nonprofit Organizations Authorized To Mail at Special Rates *(DMM Section 424.12 only)*
The purpose, function, and nonprofit status of this organization and the exempt status for Federal income tax purposes *(Check one)*

(1) ☐ Has Not Changed During Preceding 12 Months	(2) ☐ Has Changed During Preceding 12 Months	*(If changed, publisher must submit explanation of change with this statement.)*

10.	Extent and Nature of Circulation *(See instructions on reverse side)*	Average No. Copies Each Issue During Preceding 12 Months	Actual No. Copies of Single Issue Published Nearest to Filing Date
A.	Total No. Copies *(Net Press Run)*	1,819	1,765
B.	Paid and/or Requested Circulation 1. Sales through dealers and carriers, street vendors and counter sales	520	303
	2. Mail Subscription *(Paid and/or requested)*	770	890
C.	Total Paid and/or Requested Circulation *(Sum of 10B1 and 10B2)*	1,290	1,193
D.	Free Distribution by Mail, Carrier or Other Means Samples, Complimentary, and Other Free Copies	66	66
E.	Total Distribution *(Sum of C and D)*	1,356	1,259
F.	Copies Not Distributed 1. Office use, left over, unaccounted, spoiled after printing	463	506
	2. Return from News Agents	0	0
G.	TOTAL *(Sum of E, F1 and 2—should equal net press run shown in A)*	1,819	1,765

11. I certify that the statements made by me above are correct and complete	Signature and Title of Editor, Publisher, Business Manager, or Owner *[signature]* Larry Ishii Vice President

PS Form 3526, January 1991 *(See instructions on reverse)*